"FAMOUS LAST WORDS"

Apt Observations, Pleas, Curses, Benedictions, Sour Notes, Bons Mots, and Insights from People on the Brink of Departure

ALAN BISBORT

Pomegranate
SAN FRANCISCO

To Paul James Bisbort (born June 1, 2001),
my famous last word and great hope for the future.

Published by Pomegranate Communications, Inc.
Box 6099, Rohnert Park, California 94927
1-800-277-1428; www.pomegranate.com

Pomegranate Europe Ltd.
Fullbridge House, Fullbridge
Maldon, Essex CM9 4LE, England

Library of Congress Cataloging-in-Publication Data
Famous last words : apt observations, pleas, curses, benedictions, sour notes, bons mots, and insights from people on the brink of departure / [compiled by] Alan Bisbort.
p. cm.
Includes bibliographical references, name index.
ISBN 0-7649-1738-2
1. Last words. I. Bisbort, Alan, 1953– 2001021764

Pomegranate Catalog No. A606
ISBN 0-7649-1738-2

Many of the images herein were obtained from IMSI's MasterClips Collection, 1895 Francisco Blvd. East, San Rafael, CA 94901-5506, USA.

Cover and interior design by Jamison Spittler, Nevada City, California

Printed in China

10 09 08 07 06 05 04 03 02 10 9 8 7 6 5 4 3 2

CONTENTS

INTRODUCTION

The last words of the dying are like the final line of a haiku or the clue hidden among the inscrutable folds of a Zen koan. The only thing one can say with certainty about them is that all that follows in their wake is the infinite silence, the mystery of death, and the unflappable force of life. The dead have had their say, and we the living are left to ponder what their words could mean. Human existence comes together like a thunderclap in that last moment, and an agonizing question lingers: are people at the last moment visited by some particular insight denied the rest of us?

In short, the last words of the dying could mean just about anything, or they could signify absolutely nothing—meaninglessness taken to a profound level. We won't know for sure which it will be until we, too, take our places in our final exit scenes. Since most of us will be given the chance to speak our own famous last words, it might be instructive to see what some of our eminent forebears have uttered. To paraphrase Leo Tolstoy's last words, "How do the famous die?"

Some left this world in a burst of glory, one last breath of wisdom or heroism on their lips; some let their deeds do the talking; some departed ingloriously. But the chances are pretty good that even the most eloquent among them were at a loss for words when confronting the Great Beyond. Surely the true last words of most people, famous or not,

are the names of loved ones, perhaps a penitent prayer, or even a pained "Help me!" (Goethe was said to cry for "More light!" and Tallulah Bankhead for "Codeine! Bourbon!") Nonetheless, some folks left this world with some remarkable parting shots and/or lasting impressions. Included here are the words of luminaries as disparate as Malcolm X and Mata Hari, Cobain and Piaf, Jesus and Buddha—some actual, some apocryphal, some symbolic.

The famous last words of the living are another matter, and some of those are included in this collection, too. Those who spoke them went on with their lives—from Gen. Douglas MacArthur to Richard Nixon—but they were defined by these farewell statements, often to their enduring frustration. Some, like the Shah of Iran, were made to eat their words, and others lost jobs and saw their careers ruined because of them. Also included, as a counterpoint, are some idealized last words—those offered on stage, screen, and the final pages of books—and even a few appropriate epitaphs.

I don't pretend to have assembled a definitive collection out of this effort. There are hundreds of such lists, presenting thousands of alleged (and not always reliable) famous last words. The aim of this collection is to be representative and factual. That is, the famous last words are put into a factual context—with the words themselves verified by reliable sources or original texts—so that the reader might be able to make sense of them. The ideal hope, of course, is that the sharpest-minded readers will find some unifying human impulse behind all these famous last words. Those lucky few just may have stumbled upon the meaning of life.

Chapter One

On the Deathbed

"What is the answer? In that case, what is the question?"

NAME: Gertrude Stein
YEARS OF LIFE: 1874–1946
OCCUPATION: Writer

Enigmatic even to her last breath, Gertrude Stein baffled as many people as she delighted in her long literary life. After studying medicine at Johns Hopkins University in Baltimore, Stein grew bored with examinations and removed herself to Paris, where she lived for most of the rest of her life, even remaining there after the Nazis overran France. In Paris, Stein was at the center of a vibrant salon, whose habitués included the groundbreaking artists Pablo Picasso, Henri Matisse, and Georges Bracques; she later encouraged a number of young writers, such as the struggling Ernest Hemingway, to whom she uttered such choice bons mots as "Remarks are not literature." Always controversial, Stein's work (including *Three Lives, The Autobiography of Alice B. Toklas,* and *Tender Buttons*), intended as a written counterpart to Cubism, was viewed either as the product of genius or as tedious failed experiment. Alice B. Toklas, her lifelong companion, lover, and chronicler, came to Paris with Stein in 1903 and seldom left her side. She did write an autobiography, though not the one penned by Stein. Hers is *What Is Remembered* (1963); in it, Toklas reports Stein's famous last words, from her vantage point beside the famous writer's deathbed.

"Thomas Jefferson still survives."

NAME: John Adams
YEARS OF LIFE: 1735–1826
OCCUPATION: Lawyer; first vice president and second president of the United States

One of the most remarkable coincidences in American history occurred on July 4, 1826, when Thomas Jefferson and John Adams died, exactly fifty years after the Day of Independence they helped bring into existence. Two of the nation's great leaders, Adams and Jefferson were comrades during the early days of independence—Jefferson called Adams a "colossus" for his quiet strength and leadership. But they became political rivals in 1796, when Jefferson ran against Adams and his conservative Federalist Party for the presidency. Adams won that election, but Jefferson won the next one, in 1801. By 1812, they had patched up their differences and commenced a long and fruitful correspondence. Still, Adams's obsession with Jefferson continued to the deathbed. He died believing his erstwhile rival had outlived him. In fact, Jefferson had died two hours earlier; his last words were "Is it the Fourth?"

"You made one mistake. You married me."

NAME: Brendan Behan
YEARS OF LIFE: 1923–1964
OCCUPATION: Playwright; pub crawler

Brendan Behan joined the Fianna, the youth organization of the Irish Republican Army, at the age of eight, and began writing for political journals at twelve. He steeped himself in Irish history and literature, as well as the rudiments of bombmaking and beer drinking. At sixteen, he served a stint in England's Borstal Prison for carrying a bomb; at nineteen, he earned another sentence for attempting to shoot a policeman. In prison, he turned his hand, in earnest, to writing. Over the next several years, in and out of prison, Behan wrote prolifically—ribald memoirs like *Borstal Boy*; plays like *The Quare Fellow* and *The Hostage*; stories, poems, and songs. He was fond of performing the latter, well lubricated by drink, in public. By the end of his life, Behan was a sloppy drunk. Not surprisingly, he met a premature end in a Dublin hospital. In the aftermath of emergency medical treatment for liver disease, he consumed a bottle of brandy snuck into his hospital room by one of his drinking companions. This combination induced a diabetic semicoma, and a tracheotomy was performed to allow Behan to breathe more freely. His long-suffering wife, Beatrice, was at his bedside throughout the ordeal. Just before he died, Behan raised up and made the above observation—which she duly recorded years later in a memoir, *My Life with Brendan* (1973).

"No friend ever served me, and no enemy ever wronged me, whom I have not repaid in full."

NAME: Lucius Cornelius Sulla
DATES OF LIFE: 138–78 B.C.
OCCUPATION: Dictator

Sulla was a ruthless Roman consul who maintained his grip on power through a period of nearly constant foreign war and civil strife. Nonetheless, he was renowned for his devotion to wine, women, battle, and song. As the Roman historian Sallust wrote, "He lived extravagantly, yet pleasure never interfered with his duties, except that his conduct as a husband might have been more honorable." Sulla's soldiers feared but revered him. As Will Durant observed, "Living half the time on battlefields, spending the last decade of his life in civil war, he nevertheless preserved his good humor to the end, graced his brutalities with epigrams, filled Rome with laughter, made a hundred thousand enemies, achieved all his purposes, and died in bed." He also dictated these words as his epitaph.

"Behold now, brethren, decay is inherent in all component things. Work out your salvation with diligence."

NAME: Siddhartha Gautama Buddha
YEARS OF LIFE: c. 563–483 B.C.
OCCUPATION: Founder of Buddhism

He was born to a noble family called Gautama, in what is now northern India or southern Nepal, and given the name Siddhartha. By the age of nineteen, he was married and living a life of luxury and frivolity. After ten years of this, Siddhartha had a vision, prompted by the consecutive sightings of a decrepit old man, another suffering from disease, and an ascetic wanderer. Aspiring to the calm dignity of the latter, he renounced his life. Abandoning his wife and newborn baby, he gave himself over to wandering, meditation, self-denial, fasting, and study. At thirty-five, he attained to Nirvana, becoming a Buddha, or Enlightened One, and a prophet for his new religion, encapsulated in his Noble Eightfold Path. He never wavered from this path, and he was teaching it to his disciples even with his dying breath.

"I must go in, for the fog is rising."

NAME: Emily Dickinson
YEARS OF LIFE: 1830–1886
OCCUPATION: Poet

Leading a quiet and secluded life in Amherst, Massachusetts, Emily Dickinson secretly carved out a place in the top rank of world literature. Along with her contemporary, Walt Whitman, she is credited with helping to create modern American poetry. Due to her eccentricity and profound shyness, however, her fame was entirely posthumous. Only eight of her eighteen hundred poems were published in her lifetime, and she rarely left her family's house. During her final illness, from kidney disease and complications of a stroke, her mind wandered freely through her childhood. Just before making the statement above, she said, "It's already growing damp."

"Moose . . . Indian."

NAME: Henry David Thoreau
YEARS OF LIFE: 1817–1862
OCCUPATION: Pencil maker; surveyor; naturalist; writer

After his beloved brother John died of lockjaw in 1841, Henry Thoreau became what he called a "saunterer." Each day, until his own health failed, he would walk for hours among the woods and fields surrounding Concord and, later, farther afield, to Cape Cod and Maine. At the end of each "saunter," Thoreau recorded his impressions in his journals. Much of his published work emerged from these journals—posthumously. Only two books were published in his lifetime: *A Week on the Concord and Merrimac Rivers* and *Walden, or Life in the Woods.* The latter was his account of the two years and two months he lived in a hut that he had built next to Walden Pond, "watching the progress of the seasons." Not until his long final illness did Thoreau begin spending time again with members of his family back in Concord. Many of his remarkably keen insights were recorded during this illness—including, a few days before his famous last two words, the often-quoted response he made to a well-meaning aunt who asked him if he had made his peace with God: "I did not know we had ever quarrelled." Those close to him conjectured that his mention of moose and Native Americans referred to a book about the Maine woods that he had been intending to write when he became ill.

"Never sell the bones of your father and mother."

NAME: Tuekaka (Old Joseph)
YEARS OF LIFE: 1786–1871
OCCUPATION: Chief of the Nez Percé

Old Joseph said these words on his deathbed to his son, Young Joseph (1840–1904), who became the legendary Chief Joseph of the Nez Percé after his father's death. Endeavoring to make good on his father's deathbed wish, Young Joseph became a living symbol of noble resistance six years later, when he led his people on a six-month, seventeen-hundred-mile running battle with federal troops. It started when troops began a forced removal of the Nez Percé from their Oregon homeland to a refugee camp in Idaho after negotiations for the land broke down. Determined to honor his father's request, Young Joseph resisted, leading his heavily outnumbered and outgunned people into Canada, to seek refuge among the Crow people. Although Joseph engineered an amazing series of escapes, winter was coming on, his people were starving and freezing, and his "little daughter" was missing. He surrendered on October 5, 1877, with these words, "From where the sun now stands, I will fight no more forever."

"But the peasants . . . how do the peasants die?"

NAME: Leo Tolstoy
YEARS OF LIFE: 1828–1910
OCCUPATION: Writer

Count Leo Tolstoy, author of *War and Peace* and *Anna Karenina,* was a man of epic contradictions and stormy temperament. This was most obvious in his loud pronouncements about his passionate concern for the poor, the ill-treated, and the downtrodden peasants, while he himself lived on a comfortable estate. An argument with his wife about this contradiction, and a plea that they divest themselves of their wealth to live a more natural life, led to his death. Following the flare-up, he stormed off the estate, vowing to stay away forever. Eighty-two years old at the time, Tolstoy was not physically up to the challenges of the elements. He contracted pneumonia and died at the home of a railroad stationmaster in the small town of Astapovo. According to that man, these were Tolstoy's last words.

"How were the circus receipts today at Madison Square Garden?"

NAME: Phineas Taylor (P. T.) Barnum
YEARS OF LIFE: 1810–1891
OCCUPATION: Entertainment promoter

Barnum was the son of a Connecticut innkeeper and shopkeeper. He began his own career, inauspiciously, as a shopkeeper, too, while dabbling in the lottery mania of the time. Failing at this, he turned to publishing sensationalist newspapers, which earned him several libel suits and a prison term. He finally found his niche in 1835, as a showman specializing in physically unusual people, including General Tom Thumb, a dwarf, and Jenny Lind, a hugely popular singer. His best-known venue began in 1871, as the "Greatest Show on Earth," a traveling circus with menagerie and lurid sideshows. At his death, his Greatest Show was enjoying an enduringly popular stand at New York's Madison Square Garden. His main concern, as his last words attest, was always the bottom line.

"Does nobody understand?"

NAME: James Joyce
YEARS OF LIFE: 1882–1941
OCCUPATION: Writer

When James Joyce died in Zurich, Switzerland, he could very well—with this provocative question—have been summing up his writing career. After leaving Ireland in 1902, wrote Stanley Kunitz, "Joyce's history for the next quarter of a century is the history of one long struggle for publication, a struggle probably unmatched in the annals of literature." Although he completed *Dubliners* that year, it would not be published until 1914. His masterly *Ulysses* started as a story for *Dubliners* but turned into a monster of complexity; he slaved over it from 1914 until 1921 (when he wrote its famous last word, "Yes"). Censorship battles and obscenity trials held up its publication, although pirated copies exchanged hands, until 1934, when the first legally printed English-language edition was published. Joyce's last book, *Finnegans Wake* (1939), required eight years of writing, revising, and polishing before he would allow it to be published, and its lukewarm, somewhat baffled reception dogged him for the rest of his life. Indeed, it did seem that nobody understood what he had written. Additionally, during the last ten years of his life, Joyce became nearly blind; his beloved daughter went insane; and his family was uprooted by the fall of France in 1940, necessitating a reluctant move from Paris. Posthumously, Joyce has found many appreciative and understanding readers. He is also the subject of one of the finest literary biographies ever written, Richard Ellmann's *James Joyce* (1959), in which these last words are cited.

"I've made a long voyage and been to a strange country, and I've seen the dark man very close; and I don't think I was too much afraid of him, but so much of mortality still clings to me—I wanted most desperately to live and still do. . . ."

NAME: Thomas Wolfe
YEARS OF LIFE: 1900–1938
OCCUPATION: Writer

The last thing novelist Thomas Wolfe ever wrote was a short, emotional letter to his erstwhile editor and friend, Maxwell Perkins. Perkins had been the genial and brilliant guiding editorial hand behind Wolfe's first two celebrated novels, *Look Homeward, Angel* (1929) and *Of Time and the River* (1935), but they had become estranged over subsequent writings and book contracts. The friends had not spoken for three years. But when Wolfe was deathly ill in a hospital bed, his thoughts drifted back to the man who had meant so much to him. Dated August 12, 1938, the letter was snuck out against doctors' orders. Wolfe was in desperate need of rest, having contracted pneumonia on a trip out west. From his Seattle hospital room, Wolfe wrote Perkins, "I've got a hunch" that he would recover, return to the east coast, and reestablish their fruitful relationship, which he so fondly recalls in this letter. Unfortunately, the initial diagnosis of pneumonia was only half right. Wolfe had also contracted tuberculosis, which had localized in his brain. He died a month later in the same hospital bed, without having recovered the strength to write another word.

"I wish to announce the first plank in my campaign for reelection . . . we're going to have the floors in this goddamned hospital smoothed out!"

NAME: James Michael Curley
YEARS OF LIFE: 1874–1958
OCCUPATION: Politician

Colorful, charismatic, and controversial, James Curley was the consummate populist. He dominated Boston politics for over half a century, with a constituency deeply rooted in the city's large working-class Irish community. Curley held every conceivable elective office: he was mayor of Boston (four times), governor of Massachusetts, and a U.S. congressman. A great orator and tireless campaigner, he also bent the rules to further his ends. He went to prison twice, for impersonating a friend at a civil service exam and for mail fraud. After losing reelection bids for mayor in 1950 and 1954, Curley did not know when to quit. Even on the day he died (November 12, 1958), Curley was still campaigning. As he was being wheeled out of surgery, he is reported to have said these words to his son.

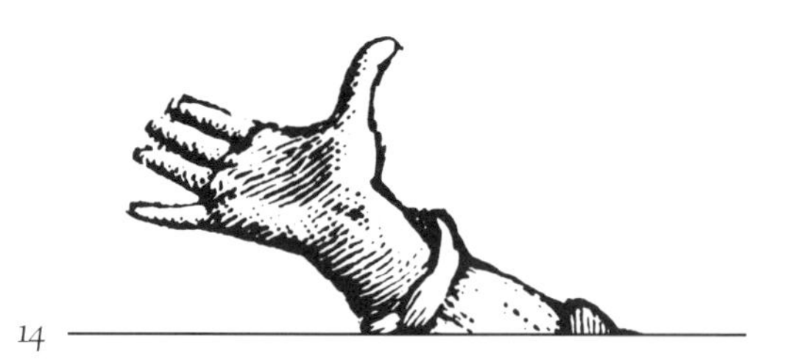

"I knew it! Born in a goddamned hotel room, and dying in a hotel room."

NAME: Eugene O'Neill
YEARS OF LIFE: 1888–1953
OCCUPATION: Playwright

Winner of the 1936 Nobel Prize in literature, O'Neill did not lead a peaceful life. As his famous last words attest, he was born in a New York City hotel room, the son of a touring actor and a tormented, drug-addicted mother. Although he railed against the insecurities and deprivations of an itinerant childhood, O'Neill not only drifted into a career in the theater but took up a life as restless as his father's had been. Despite popular success and critical acclaim for plays like *Anna Christie* and *Desire Under the Elms,* O'Neill was dogged by alcoholism, depression, and foul childhood memories. These latter ghosts were given eternal life with the posthumous publication of his starkly autobiographical *Long Day's Journey into Night.* O'Neill spent his last year and a half living in a suite at the Hotel Shelton in Boston. His third wife, Carlotta, with him when he died, reported these as his last words.

"Why? Why not?"

NAME: Timothy Leary
YEARS OF LIFE: 1920–1996
OCCUPATION: Psychologist; provocateur

These words, spoken on May 31, 1996, were Timothy Leary's last upon this earthly plane, as reported in the *Los Angeles Times.* The media were at his bedside, along with twenty friends and family members, at Leary's invitation. A year before, when he had learned that he had inoperable prostate cancer, Leary had declared that his death would be on his own terms. He turned it into a media event, not unlike the many other acts of defiance that characterized his career as a maverick. (Richard Nixon called him "the most dangerous man in America.") Leary's initial plan was to commit suicide and broadcast it live over the Internet and then have his head severed and cryogenically frozen in a space helmet. The illness overtook him, however, and so he had to be content with the knowledge that his cremated remains would be blasted off into outer space half a year later—again, to much media fanfare.

"All the damn fool things you do in life you pay for."

NAME: Edith Piaf (born Edith Giovanna Gassion)
YEARS OF LIFE: 1915–1963
OCCUPATION: Singer; actress

Edith Piaf was ill fated, it seems, from the start. She was abandoned at birth by her mother, a Parisian café singer, and father, a circus acrobat. At the age of three, she contracted meningitis and was blind for four years. As a young girl, she turned to the *chanson* (French balladry) and sang those often tragic songs in the streets of Paris. She was discovered by a cabaret owner, who had her change her name to Piaf ("sparrow"). She eventually became world famous for her distinctive singing style, which literally moved audiences to tears. After years of international touring, and chronic ill health, she returned to Paris, where she contracted pneumonia. She knew she was dying when she offered this piece of advice to her sister, who was at her bedside.

"Ne frustra vixisse videar." (May I not seem to have lived in vain.)

NAME: Tycho Brahe
YEARS OF LIFE: 1546–1601
OCCUPATION: Astronomer

After his great success in 1572 of discovering a new star in the constellation of Cassiopeia, Tycho Brahe convinced King Frederick II to give him an island off the coast of Copenhagen. There he set up a castle, gardens, a library, a laboratory, and an observatory. Over the next two decades, he studied the origin of comets and the movement of the sun and moon, and cataloged 777 stars. After Frederick's heir cut off his funds, Brahe went to Prague as a guest of Emperor Rudolf II. He set up another laboratory, hired Johann Kepler as an assistant, and was on the verge of setting down his life's work in a coherent theory of the heavens. But, his balloon burst—actually, his bladder erupted during a meal—and he lay on his deathbed for eleven days, while his faithful assistant recorded his every utterance. According to Kepler, these were Brahe's last words. The orator at his funeral sagely observed that Brahe "coveted nothing but time."

"I've just had eighteen straight whiskies. I think that's the record."

NAME: Dylan Thomas
YEARS OF LIFE: 1914–1953
OCCUPATION: Poet

Before alcohol robbed him of his remarkable talent, Dylan Thomas wrote some of the finest verse in the English language of his day. Among his classic poems are "The Force That Through the Green Fuse Drives the Flower," "Fern Hill," and "Do Not Go Gentle into That Good Night." His gift for language extended to poetic plays like *Under Milk Wood* and memoirs (*A Child's Christmas in Wales*); his story collections include *Portrait of the Artist as a Young Dog.* Thomas spent his whole adult life in dire financial straits, partly due to his weakness for the bottle. Because of the former issue, Thomas embarked on wildly successful speaking tours of the United States, which were consistently colored by the latter: he liked to boast that he was "the drunkest man in the world." On what would be his final U.S. speaking tour, Thomas found himself in a drinking contest in New York City. These were reported to be his last words before he passed out, never to reawaken.

"You can't kill this tough Jew."

NAME: Rod Serling
YEARS OF LIFE: 1925–1975
OCCUPATION: Writer; host of *The Twilight Zone*

Rod Serling was one of the giants of television during its golden age of live broadcasting. He got his start as a writer with *Kraft Television Theater* and *Playhouse 90*, penning award-winning screenplays, among which was "Requiem for a Heavyweight." In 1959, he created *The Twilight Zone*, a hugely popular series that ran until 1965. *The Twilight Zone* presented original dramas that were alternately science fiction, fantasy, surrealistic, and visionary, but always thought provoking. The opening narration for the premiere is now one of the most familiar in TV history: "The land that lies between science and superstition, between the pit of man's fears and the summit of his knowledge. . . . " Serling went on to other challenges, including teaching, but his health was ruined by heavy smoking, and he suffered a series of heart attacks. After his second one, he wrote this note from his hospital bed to former *Twilight Zone* colleague Owen Comora. He died during open-heart surgery soon afterward.

"Strike the tent!"

NAME: Robert E. Lee
YEARS OF LIFE: 1807–1870
OCCUPATION: Commander of the Confederate military

After the Civil War, the commander of the defeated Confederate forces promoted reconciliation with the same quiet dignity he had displayed throughout his military career. In 1865 Lee moved to Lexington, Virginia, to become president of Washington College (later renamed, in his honor, Washington and Lee). Leaving church one day, he suffered a stroke and lingered for several days, mostly mute and in great pain. Just before he died, Lee broke his silence to shout what sounded like battle orders. First, he said, "Tell Hill he must come up!", and then he said, "Strike the tent!" He died the next morning, never to speak another word.

"Pull up the shades; I don't want to go home in the dark."

NAME: O. Henry (born William Sydney Porter)
YEARS OF LIFE: 1862–1910
OCCUPATION: Writer

William Porter took the pen name O. Henry after he had been imprisoned in Ohio in 1897 for bank fraud. His life to that point was itinerant, raw, adventurous, and full of hard drinking. After his release from prison, he eventually drifted to New York City, where he was known to haunt the streets around Gramercy Park between writing and drinking binges. During these years, O. Henry maintained an almost superhuman writing pace; best-selling volumes of his stories—*Cabbages and Kings, The Four Million, Waifs and Strays, Hearts of the West, The Trimmed Lamp and Other Stories, The Gentle Grafter,* and *The Voice of the City*—were all published between 1905 and 1908. He reportedly consumed, on average, two quarts of whiskey a day. Debilitated by years of hard living, he contracted tuberculosis. His final bout with the disease began at the Caledonia Hotel in New York; two days later, he was moved to the Polyclinic Hospital on East 35th Street. He knew he was dying, of course, and his last words were this request to the attending nurse, paraphrasing a popular song of the time.

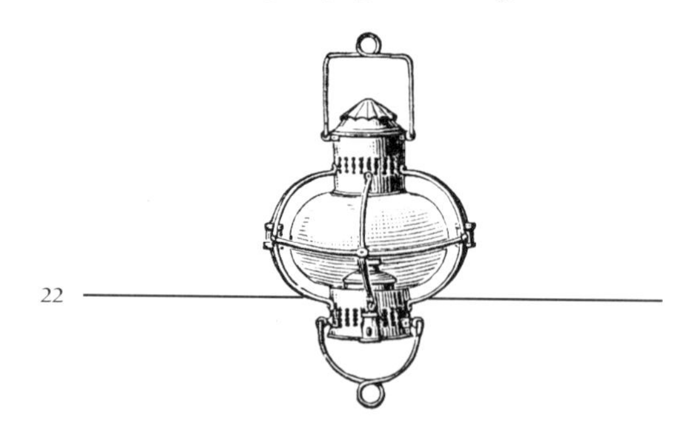

"Sixty-four thousand, nine hundred and twenty-eight."

NAME: Neal Cassady
YEARS OF LIFE: 1926–1968
OCCUPATION: Drifter; Merry Prankster

A Beat Generation legend and the model for Dean Moriarty in Jack Kerouac's *On the Road,* Neal Cassady clung to his role as "the holy goof," finding kindred spirits among Ken Kesey's Merry Pranksters. But his con man tricks, personal intensity, and prodigious drug intake had burned all his bridges. In February 1968, after getting out of jail for outstanding traffic warrants, he left San Francisco and took a train to Celaya, Mexico. Leaving his bag at the Celaya train station, he took a taxi to the house of a young lover in San Miguel de Allende. The next day, he told his companion that he planned to walk back to Celaya to retrieve his "magic bag," counting the railroad ties as he went. On the way, he came upon a wedding party, where he washed down a number of Seconals with pulque. Thus fortified, he set out to count the railroad ties. He was found on the railroad tracks. The local Indians who had found him claim that his last words were "64,928," apparently the subtotal of his count in progress.

"Let not my body be sent to England. Here let my bones molder. Lay me in the first corner without pomp or nonsense."

NAME: Lord Byron (George Gordon Byron)
YEARS OF LIFE: 1788–1824
OCCUPATION: Poet

While aiding Greek insurgents on the Ionian island of Cephalonia, Byron was stricken with convulsions and began foaming at the mouth. After being treated with leeches, his condition improved, but he soon came down with chills, and then a fever. His illness (which some have conjectured was syphilis) was clearly mortal, and his chief physician, Dr. Julius Millingen, did not leave his bedside during his last few days. The doctor recorded that Byron never brought up religion, or the afterlife, although he heard the poet say, "Shall I sue for mercy?" and then, after a pause, "Come, come; no weakness! Let's be a man to the end." His last recorded words were these instructions, given to Dr. Millingen. Unable to honor his last request, the doctor had his body embalmed in 180 pounds of "spirits" and shipped to London. When a petition to bury him in Poets Corner of Westminster Abbey was refused, Byron's body was laid to rest in the churchyard at Newstead Abbey, his baronial seat.

"Listen . . . I am singing a little song for you. The whole world came between us."

NAME: John Reed
YEARS OF LIFE: 1887–1920
OCCUPATION: Poet; journalist; revolutionary

Depicted as a playboy-revoutionary in the film *Reds,* John Reed was the "golden boy" of Greenwich Village, a bohemian poet to whom his famous mentor Lincoln Steffens said, "You can do anything." Prodded by idealism and superhuman energy, Reed began organizing workers and writing for *The Masses,* the most influential leftist journal of its time. When the Russian Revolution broke out, Reed dove at the chance to see this flame of ideological idealism firsthand. He went to Russia, wrote a famous account (*Ten Days That Shook the World*), and became something of a hero of (and a potent symbol for) the Communist cause. His wife, the poet Louise Bryant, disguised herself as a sailor and joined Reed in Moscow. But he contracted influenza and typhus, and, despite four doctors, two consulting physicians, a surgeon, and nurses attending him night and day, he died in Marinsky Hospital. These were his last words, spoken to Bryant, who was at his bedside. Reed is the only American buried in the Kremlin.

"Try to be forgotten. Go live in the country. Stay in mourning for two years, then remarry, but choose somebody decent."

NAME: Alexander Pushkin
YEARS OF LIFE: 1799–1837
OCCUPATION: Poet

Alexander Pushkin holds the same importance in Russian literature as William Shakespeare does in English literature. The prolific author of *Eugene Onegin, Boris Godunov,* and *The Captain's Daughter* (among many other works), Pushkin wrote in nearly every major genre to create, almost single-handedly, a Russian national literature. On the morning of his fatal wounding, Pushkin rose and worked in his study as if it were just another day. He felt so little concern that he did not even tell his wife, Natalya, or his four children that he was taking part in a duel. His opponent was a vain, dissolute young man, Baron Georges Heckeren d'Anthes, the adopted son of the Dutch minister in St. Petersburg. Heckerin was married to Natalya's sister, but it was rumored that he had made lewd overtures to Natalya. A series of accusatory letters exchanged hands, and Heckerin, claiming offense, challenged Pushkin to a duel. The poet accepted and—eerily presaged by a scene in his own epic *Eugene Onegin*—was mortally wounded, although he didn't die until two days later. In those days he received a steady stream of family, friends, and neighbors to his bedside. Among his last words were these to Natalya. She took him up on his suggestion, marrying an army officer named Lanskoi and living until 1863.

"I want to get mumbo-jumbo out of the world."

NAME: William Morris
YEARS OF LIFE: 1834–1896
OCCUPATION: Printer; artist; writer; socialist; decorator

William Morris was blessed and cursed with remarkable energy, unable to rest until he accomplished his goal of revolutionizing Victorian English society into a form of socialism through his art and literature. He cofounded an interior design firm that manufactured wallpaper, furniture, and other items that transformed the taste of the British people into what became the Arts and Crafts movement. He founded Kelmscott Press to express his principles through book design. He wrote revolutionary pamphlets, edited a progressive literary magazine, established the Society for the Protection of Ancient Buildings, lectured, and wrote stories and poems that are classics of fantastical literature. Morris died surrounded by all he loved: illuminated manuscripts, his library, his Kelmscott House, friends, family, and admirers. He whispered his last words to his family doctor, who said that Morris "died a victim of his enthusiasm for spreading the principles of Socialism." Another attending physician opined, "The disease is simply being William Morris, and having done more work than most ten men."

"Go to the rising sun; my sun is setting."

NAME: Marcus Aurelius (Marcus Annius Aurelius Antoninus)
YEARS OF LIFE: 121–180
OCCUPATION: Emperor; philosopher

Marcus Aurelius was educated by tutors in rhetoric and poetry, but, at the age of eleven, he became smitten with Stoicism, a philosophy that demanded rigid discipline, hard work, and self-denial. Marcus became emperor in 161, commanding deep respect from his court and his subjects, despite all manner of national misfortune—including flood, famine, earthquakes, fires, plagues of insects, and war. Indeed, few Roman emperors enjoyed the sort of unassailable moral authority that he did. Marcus was a great philosopher whose meditations included this one on death: "Pass, then, through this little space of time conformably with nature, and end thy journeys in content, just as an olive falls when it is ripe, blessing the nature that produced it, and thanking the tree on which it grew." Thus it was, as he lay dying, that he pondered the reign of his nineteen-year-old son and heir, Commodus. The officer of the guard came to Marcus's chamber to ask for the day's watchword, and he made the answer above. The "rising sun" was Commodus, whose personal habits (and eventual rule) were as corrupt as Marcus's were incorruptible. Commodus drank, gambled, spent lavishly, inflicted wanton cruelty on cripples and "women devotees of Isis," and kept a harem of three hundred women and three hundred boys.

"I never felt happy in this life. That is why I left home. My mother would have married me to someone ordinary and I could never have stood it, Irma. A decent woman has to get on in the world."

NAME: Eva Maria (Evita) Duarte de Peron
YEARS OF LIFE: 1919–1952
OCCUPATION: Actress; wife of Argentina president Juan Domingo Peron

After saying these words to her maid, Evita Peron fell into a coma; she died a few hours later, on July 26, 1952. She had cancer, and, over the course of her long illness, she wrote feverishly. Her lengthy will ended, "My last words shall be as my first ones; I want to live eternally with Peron and my people, God will forgive me if I prefer to remain with them because he, too, is with the poor and I have always understood that in each *descamisado* God was asking me for love which I never withheld." Among her last wishes was a rambling handwritten note that warned, "If God doesn't help all the peoples, millions of workers, women, children, and old people will be exploited by these evil men." Although she held no official position, Peron wielded vast power in Argentina, and while she was revered by millions of poor Argentines, she made powerful enemies. After her death, her body was embalmed and put on public display. Her husband was deposed and exiled in 1955, and her body disappeared. But it reappeared—miraculously, some said—and was redisplayed in the 1970s. Evita Peron's legend was assured.

"There is nothing more I should do to it now, and therefore I am not likely to be more ready to go than at this moment."

NAME: Ulysses S. Grant
YEARS OF LIFE: 1822–1885
OCCUPATION: Military leader; president of the United States

Grant didn't speak these words with his dying breath; he wrote them a week before he died. Still, they indicate his state of mind in his last hours. Grant was suffering terribly from inoperable cancer, and his doctor had told him it was imminently fatal. He had retreated to a summer cottage in the Adirondacks to write his memoirs, in hopes that the proceeds from them would help take care of his family after his death. (The previous year, he had been bankrupted by a financial scam.) Having completed his memoirs, Grant wrote his doctor to tell him that he was prepared to go. Mark Twain published Grant's memoirs. It was one of the few good financial investments that Twain, a legendarily bad money manager, ever made. The book sold half a million copies, and Grant's family was well cared for after his death.

"Will you do one last thing for me? Some time, when the team's up against it and things aren't breaking right, tell the boys to go out and win just one for the Gipper. Wherever I'll be, Coach, I'll know about it and it'll make me very happy."

NAME: George Gipp
YEARS OF LIFE: 1895–1920
OCCUPATION: All-American halfback

George Gipp was a natural athlete who, although he never played football until he went to college at Notre Dame, became a gridiron legend. In his four years at Notre Dame, the team won twenty-seven games, lost only two, and tied three. Gipp scored twenty-one touchdowns on offense; on defense, he never allowed a pass to be completed to the man he was guarding. During a game against Illinois in November 1920, he contracted a streptococcic infection of the throat, which worsened in his final game against Northwestern. He was sent to the hospital, where he died December 14, 1920. Notre Dame football coach Knute Rockne, visiting Gipp in the hospital, has recorded these as his star's dying words. He used them in his speeches at halftime, to inspire his team when they were behind on the scoreboard.

Chapter Two

On the Gallows/ On the Firing Line

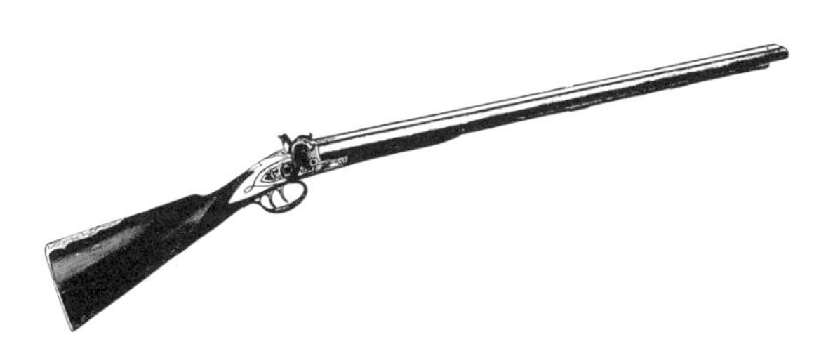

"Father, into Your hands I commit My spirit."

NAME: Jesus of Nazareth
YEARS OF LIFE: 1–33
OCCUPATION: Religious leader

For many people, these are the most important parting words in world history, but the Bible differs in its accounts of Jesus's last utterance. According to the Gospels of Mark (15:34) and Matthew (27:46), it was "My God, My God, why have You forsaken Me?", said in His ninth hour on the cross, although both disciples relate that moments later "Jesus cried out with a loud voice," then breathed his last. In the Gospel of John, His last words in this spirit form are recorded as "If I will that he remain till I come, what is that to you?" According to the Gospel of Luke (23:33–56), as Jesus was placed on His cross between two criminals, he said, "Father, forgive them, for they know not what they do." During Christ's sixth hour on the cross, one of the onlookers asked Jesus to remember him when He entered the Kingdom of God, to which Jesus replied, "Today shalt thou be with Me in Paradise." In His ninth hour, Jesus called out the above (verse 46), making these his last words in fleshly form on Earth.

"Crito, I owe a cock to Asclepius; will you remember to pay the debt?"

NAME: Socrates
YEARS OF LIFE: c. 470–399 B.C.
OCCUPATION: Philosopher

Socrates professed to be both an Athenian patriot and a "citizen of the world." A constant and familiar presence on the streets, in the marketplace, and in the gymnasia of Athens, he wielded huge influence as a free-thinking political gadfly. Because he left no written works, accounts of his life are provided by Xenophon, and summations of his philosophy are recorded by his student Plato, who seems to have hung on his every word. One thing is clear from these accounts: Socrates was an unaffected and honest man. It is entirely within character for him to remember, just before his death, the debt of a chicken owed to one of his friends. Plato's account of his last days, in *Phaedo*, indicates that Socrates accepted his death sentence—for "denying the gods recognized by the state" and "corrupting the young"—with cheerfulness and peace of mind.

"Et tu, Brute? Then fall, Caesar!"

NAME: Julius Caesar
YEARS OF LIFE: 100–44 B.C.
OCCUPATION: Emperor

In his 1599 play based on the assassination of the Roman emperor Julius Caesar—from which these famous last words are drawn—William Shakespeare stuck closely to historical fact. In addition to the many other contemporaneous plays that depicted scenes of Caesar's murder, Shakespeare used Plutarch's *Lives of the Noble Grecians and Romaines . . .*, an important edition of which was translated into English by Thomas North in 1579. According to Plutarch (46?–120?)—and as reflected in Shakespeare's play—Caesar was killed by freedom-loving conspirators led by Cassius and Casca, who feared his increasingly tyrannical power. Brutus, one of Caesar's dearest friends, reluctantly joined the plot out of a sense of duty to the republic. Fighting desperately for his life, Caesar sustained "three and twenty wounds upon his body"; when he saw Brutus "with his sword drawen in his hand, then he pulled his gowne over his head, and made no more reisistaunce."

"What an artist dies in me!"

NAME: Nero
YEARS OF LIFE: 37–68
OCCUPATION: Emperor

Nero was orphaned at age three, his father having died of natural causes and his mother having been banished by her brother Caligula. He obtained the throne at fourteen when his mother, returned from exile, poisoned Claudius. While he was a precocious youth, given to artistic enthusiasms and open-mindedness, his erratic reign was marked by intrigue, murder, and increasingly weird and decadent behavior, which may have included responsibility for the burning of Rome in 64. Popular dissatisfaction led to his overthrow in 68, and he went into a brief exile a few miles from Rome. A sentence of death was passed in absentia by the Roman senate, but Nero committed suicide with poison before it could be carried out. These were his last words—entirely in character—according to accounts by Tacitus and Suetonius.

"Let's do it."

NAME: Gary Mark Gilmore
YEARS OF LIFE: 1940–1977
OCCUPATION: Career criminal; convicted murderer

Gilmore was the last person in the United States to be executed by firing squad, on January 17, 1977, in the Utah State Prison. According to Norman Mailer's "true-life novel," *The Executioner's Song* (1979), Gilmore demanded to have his death sentence carried out rather than spend the remainder of his life in prison. At the time of his execution, Gilmore had been awake for twenty-four hours; he was sedated and strapped to a chair in front of the executioners' blind. When the warden asked him if he had anything to say, according to Mailer, "Gary wanted to say something good and dignified and clever, but couldn't think of anything profound. The drugs had left him too dead. Rather than say nothing, he did his best to say it very clear, 'Let's do it'."

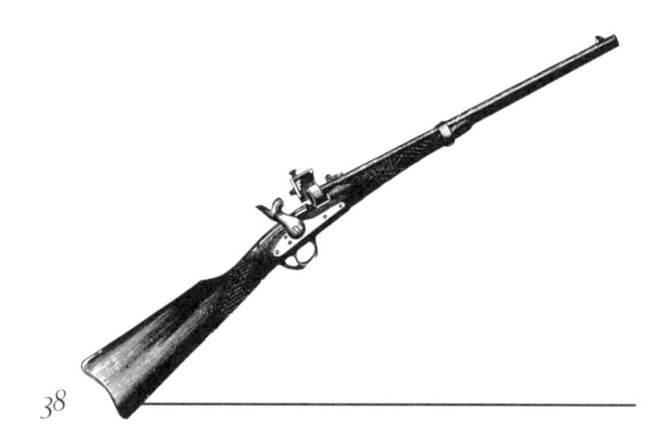

"There ain't nobody gonna shoot me."

NAME: Lee Harvey Oswald
YEARS OF LIFE: 1939–1963
OCCUPATION: Suspected assassin

In the chaotic hours after John Kennedy was killed in Dallas, a number of suspects were arrested, including the prime suspect, Lee Harvey Oswald. While in custody, Oswald repeatedly insisted he was "a patsy," but was never able to give a full testimony. Two days after his arrest, on Sunday, November 24, 1963, Oswald was to be moved from his cell in City Hall to county jail. This transfer was to take place by car, leaving from the City Hall basement, which—because the media had been tipped off—was packed with reporters and onlookers. One of the onlookers, a small-time hoodlum named Jack Ruby, shot Oswald point-blank during the transfer, claiming to want revenge for Mrs. Kennedy and her two children. According to Detective James Leavelle, who was handcuffed to Oswald, these were the prime suspect's last words.

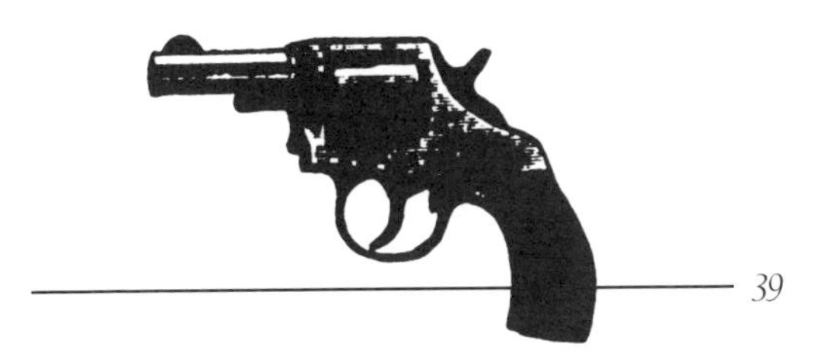

"Shoot, you coward, you're going to kill a man."

NAME: Ernesto (Che) Guevara
YEARS OF LIFE: 1928–1967
OCCUPATION: Revolutionary

An enduring icon of leftist idealism, flamboyant rebellion, and bravery, the Argentine-born Che Guevara devoted his short but brilliant career to the cause of world revolution against colonialism and capitalism. A professed Marxist-Leninist, he was a restless individual given to impassioned impulses and quixotic causes. After helping Fidel Castro overthrow Cuban dictator Fulgencio Batista in 1959, Guevara left to pursue his dream of global revolt. In 1964, he sent armed followers to aid a leftist uprising in Argentina; in 1965, he personally led a rebellion in the Congo; and in 1966–1967, he did likewise in Bolivia. All were failures, and he was captured during the Bolivian campaign, in hopeless retreat and nearly starved to death in a mountain ravine. Witnesses to his execution the next day (October 9) claim these to be his last words, spoken to Mario Teran, the Bolivian soldier who was ordered to shoot him.

"Death is nothing, nor life either, for that matter. To die, to sleep, to pass into nothingness, what does it matter? Everything is an illusion."

NAME: Mata Hari (Margaretha Geertruida Zelle)
YEARS OF LIFE: 1876–1917
OCCUPATION: Dancer; spy

Dutch-born Margaretha Zelle was much better at attracting public attention (and military men) than she was at spying. Her first conquest was Captain Campbell MacLeod, a Scotsman in the Dutch colonial army whom she married in 1897. She lived with him in Java and Sumatra, developing an interest in East Indian dance. After their divorce, she moved to Paris and began dancing professionally, and often nude, which ensured instant stardom. She changed her stage name from Lady MacLeod to Mata Hari—the Malay expression for "eye of the day," or "sun." During World War I, she first agreed to spy on France for Germany, then agreed to spy on Germany for France. Eventually, she was arrested, tried, and sentenced to death by the French. On October 15, 1917, she faced the firing squad. Her last words, spoken to a nun, reflected the Eastern mysticism with which she had once been infatuated.

"I only regret that I have but one life to lose for my country."

NAME: Nathan Hale
YEARS OF LIFE: 1755–1776
OCCUPATION: Revolutionary

Hale, a Connecticut schoolteacher, joined an American regiment when hostilities with the British began in early 1776. After serving in the siege of Boston in 1776, Hale was commissioned as a captain and went to New York, where he participated in a daring capture of a British provision sloop right under the guns of a royal man-of-war. Disguised as a Dutch schoolteacher, he boarded a ship of the British fleet to gather intelligence. He was caught while returning, summarily tried, and sentenced to be hanged. At Hale's execution, his request for a Bible and a minister were denied. His last words, upon being fitted with the noose, formed the ringing pronouncement that has secured his enshrinement as an American hero and martyr.

"I will die like a true-blue rebel. Don't waste any time in mourning—organize."

NAME: Joe Hill
YEARS OF LIFE: 1879–1915
OCCUPATION: Labor organizer; songwriter

Joe Hill was an organizer for the Industrial Workers of the World (IWW, also known as "Wobblies"), which envisioned all industrial laborers in every country organized in "One Big Union." Consequently, anyone affiliated with the IWW was considered a threat to the captains of capitalism. Because Hill was also a songwriter and singer, he had garnered international notoriety, and his rallying songs appeared in IWW publications and the Wobbly compendium, *The Little Red Song Book.* With such a high and radical profile, Hill was a sitting duck for legal railroading. Not surprisingly, he was accused of murdering a Salt Lake City grocer during a robbery; his trial was swiftly conducted, and he was sentenced to death by firing squad. Despite worldwide protests, Hill was executed November 18, 1915. His last message, telegraphed to fellow IWW organizer Bill Haywood, was this simple, stirring exhortation.

"The paper burns, but the words fly free."

NAME: Akiba ben Joseph
YEARS OF LIFE: c. 40–135
OCCUPATION: Rabbi; *tannaim*

Akiba ben Joseph was a much beloved rabbi and *tannaim* (expositor) of the Jewish law in a village called Jamnia. He did not learn to read until he was forty; then, after fifteen years of intensive study, he opened his own school under a fig tree in his village, attracting many students. Akiba was a living textbook of the Jewish law—vital to his people during the Diaspora—but he also wrote down everything he knew. During the Jews' last great uprising against the Romans to reclaim their homeland, Akiba was sentenced to death at the age of ninety-five. His written Torah was burned before his eyes, just before he was killed, and his insistence that "the words fly free" referred to the fact that Jewish law was also orally passed down. As he died, he offered Judaism's basic tenet: "Hear, O Israel! The Lord is our God, the Lord is one."

"Standing, as I do, in the view of God and eternity I realize that patriotism is not enough. I must have no hatred or bitterness towards anyone."

NAME: Edith Louisa Cavell
YEARS OF LIFE: 1865–1915
OCCUPATION: Nurse; suspected spy

Edith Louisa Cavell was an American Red Cross nurse stationed in Belgium at the peak of the German atrocities that took place there (gruesomely played upon by British propagandists). For aiding the escape of several anti-German agents, Cavell was condemned to death by the Germans and shot by a firing squad in Belgium on October 12, 1915. Her death was useful to the war effort, increasing hostility to the Germans and eventually helping to draw America into the conflict. Among the best-known and most widely disseminated images of the "murder of Edith Cavell" was a lithograph created by George Bellows that depicted her as a latter-day Joan of Arc. According to the chaplain who was by her side just before her execution by German firing squad, these were Cavell's last words.

"Thou wilt show my head to the people; it is worth showing."

NAME: Georges-Jacques Danton
YEARS OF LIFE: 1759–1794
OCCUPATION: Lawyer; revolutionary

One of the driving forces of the French Revolution, Danton was a member of the Executive Council that replaced the overthrown monarchy. Danton was a contradiction in terms, and, as Will and Ariel Durant wrote, "None of them could make him out: he organized for war and negotiated for peace; he roared like a lion and talked of mercy; he fought for the Revolution and helped some royalists to escape from France." Ultimately, like many during the Terror, Danton came under the fatal suspicion of his most powerful rival, Robespierre. After Danton advised an end to the killing ("Let us leave something to the guillotine of opinion"), his goose was cooked. Exhausted from four years of violence, he said, "I am sick of the human race." Before being beheaded at the Place de la Revolution, Danton predicted (correctly), "Vile Robespierre! The scaffold claims you too. You will follow me."

"O sancta simplicitas!" (*O holy simplicity!*)

NAME: John Huss (or Hus)
YEARS OF LIFE: c. 1372–1415
OCCUPATION: Priest

John of Husinetz was the most famous churchman in Prague at a time when the Roman Catholic Church was under attack for its corruption. Huss, as head of the Bethlehem Chapel in Prague, was one of Bohemia's loudest critics of Rome, calling Pope John XXIII a "moneygrubber" and "Antichrist" for selling indulgences to finance his bloody wars. Huss was excommunicated but kept preaching. He wrote that Christ, not the pope, was the head of the Church, and the Bible, not the pope, was the final word ("To rebel against an erring pope is to obey Christ."). He also said that the Church should own no worldly goods. Huss refused to abjure his teachings and writings. Burned at the stake on July 6, 1415, he sang hymns while the flames consumed his body.

"Come in front, and light it before my face; if I had feared death I should never have come here."

NAME: Jerome of Prague
YEARS OF LIFE: c. 1370–1416
OCCUPATION: Priest

Jerome was the leading defender of the reform-minded Catholic priest John Huss. During Huss's excommunication and imprisonment, Jerome continued to disseminate and defend his friend's teachings. After Huss was burned at the stake, Jerome recanted his "heresies," but he was sent to prison anyway. In his cell he began to reconsider his recantation, demanding a hearing before the papal-sanctioned church assembly. Before he could state his case, he was again asked to answer to the original charges. He gave one of the most impassioned indictments of church fallibility ever recorded: "And yet you are men, not gods; mortals, not eternal; you are liable to error. . . ." He refused to retract his defense of John Huss; on May 30, 1416, he was burned at the stake on the same spot as his mentor. When the executioner went to light the pyre behind him, Jerome made his famous last request.

"No one shall set the sea between me and my Church. I did not come here to run away: anyone who wants me may find me."

NAME: Thomas à Becket
YEARS OF LIFE: c. 1118–1170
OCCUPATION: Archbishop of Canterbury

Before being appointed Archbishop of Canterbury in 1162, Becket was secretary of state and close friend and adviser to King Henry II. When he became archbishop, he renounced his old ways and proclaimed the clergy exempt from civil courts—that is, the priests and their clerks were above the law. This put him in direct conflict, and in a power struggle, with the king, who wanted to eliminate the rampant corruption in the ecclesiastical courts. After eight years of intrigues, an exasperated Henry angrily addressed his Normandy court, berating his "lazy servants" for having not done him "right" by Becket's "affront." On December 29, 1170, four knights killed Becket at Canterbury. Becket uttered his famous last words after having sustained three deep sword wounds. Pope Alexander canonized Becket in 1173, and his shrine at Canterbury became the most popular place of pilgrimage in Christendom.

"A gentler and more merciful prince there never was, and to me he was ever a good, a gentle, and a sovereign lord."

NAME: Anne Boleyn
YEARS OF LIFE: 1507–1536
OCCUPATION: Wife of King Henry VIII

King Henry VIII's second wife, Anne Boleyn, was partly responsible for the final break between the Church of England and the Catholic Church in Rome. Actually, the break was caused by the pope not granting Henry a divorce from his first wife, Catherine, who was unable to produce a male heir; he wed the much younger Anne without the papal blessing. Anne's first child was a girl (later Queen Elizabeth), which further disappointed Henry. After three years of marriage, he used the rumors of Anne's infidelity (not just with the Earl of Northumberland but with her own brother) as a means of disposing of her, too. She and her brother were found guilty of incest and adultery and sentenced to death by beheading. Upon hearing that the executioner was capable of delivering the blade quickly and painlessly, Anne said, "the executioner I have heard to be very good, and I have a little neck." Just before her beheading, Anne addressed those assembled with these generous words about her husband.

"I pray you, Mr. Lieutenant, see me safe up, and for my coming down let me shift for myself."

NAME: Thomas More
YEARS OF LIFE: 1478–1535
OCCUPATION: Lord Chancellor of England

Thomas More, author of *Utopia,* was a favorite of the English royal court. Like Henry VIII, for whom he served as lord chancellor (the second highest rank in England), More was a staunch Catholic. However, when Henry split with the Vatican over his marriage to Anne Boleyn, Sir Thomas was torn between loyalty to king and loyalty to pope—and to God. Rather than repudiate the papacy, as most of the English clergy had already done to appease Henry, More remained silent. His refusal to renounce Rome was seen as a betrayal by the king. He was charged with treason, tried, sentenced to be "hanged, drawn, and quartered." The king, out of fondness for More, changed the sentence to a less "cruel" beheading. As he mounted the scaffold, More nearly fell on the shaking platform. Turning to a king's officer, he made this last request. His head was later mounted, as an object lesson, on London Bridge.

"My son must never forget his father's last words, which I expressly repeat to him: 'Never seek to avenge my death.'"

NAME: Marie Antoinette
YEARS OF LIFE: 1755–1793
OCCUPATION: Queen of France; wife of Louis XVI

During her ordeal of mourning for the execution of her husband, Marie Antoinette won back a bit of popular regard, undoing some of the perception of her as a callous, extravagant queen. Her imprisonment and the dignity she displayed at her humiliating trial before the Revolutionary Tribunal contributed to this, as did the calm with which she took her death sentence. On the eve of her beheading, Marie Antoinette wrote a letter to her sister-in-law Elisabeth, who had been entrusted to care for her daughter, Marie-Therese, and son, Louis-Charles, the dauphin (whom she considered King Louis XVII). Sadly, the letter was intercepted at court and never delivered. It was given to Robespierre, and only after his death was it found among his papers. It is said that, climbing the scaffold to the guillotine, Marie Antoinette stepped on the foot of the executioner, begged his pardon, and said, "I didn't do it on purpose."

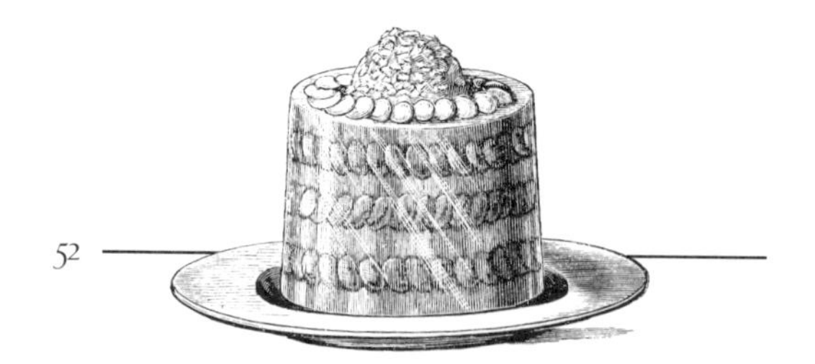

"O Liberty, what crimes are committed in your name!"

NAME: Jeanne-Manon Roland
YEARS OF LIFE: 1754–1793
OCCUPATION: Member of the royal court of King Louis XVI

In the wake of Marie Antoinette's beheading, the French Revolutionary Tribunal began issuing death sentences at a rate of seven per day. Among those sentenced was Jeanne-Manon Roland, wife of the royal minister of the interior. After her husband escaped arrest by the Tribunal's forces, she was put in prison, where she began writing her memoirs, called *Appel d'impartiale posterite.* Roland drifted into reveries about happier times, although she was always pulled back to her current miseries. She finally gave up working on the memoirs, writing, "Never can history paint these dreadful times, or the monsters that fill them with their barbarities . . . What Rome or Babylon ever equaled Paris? . . . How long must I remain a witness to the desolation of my native land, the degradation of my countrymen?" On her way to the guillotine, she saw a statue of Liberty sculpted by David. These words were inspired by her final glance at that statue.

"I just want to say I hold no hard feelings. You people are sending me to a better world than this ever was."

NAME: Richard Eugene Hickock
YEARS OF LIFE: 1922–1965
OCCUPATION: Drifter; murderer

On November 15, 1959, the Clutter family of Holcomb, Kansas, was brutally murdered by knife and shotgun. The account of this multiple murder and its consequences was grippingly recounted in Truman Capote's "non-fiction novel" *In Cold Blood* (1965). The first of the two men executed for the four murders was Richard Hickock. Capote chronicles his last minutes with almost surgical precision, describing the hangman ("reminiscent of a turkey buzzard huffing"), the conversation of the witnesses, Hickock's last meal (shrimp, French fries, garlic bread, ice cream, strawberries with whipped cream), the "prayer-murmuring" chaplain, Hickock's eyes ("enfeebled by half a decade of cell shadows"), and the "delicate black mask tied round the prisoner's eyes." Soon after Hickock's execution, his partner, Perry Smith, was hung from the same gallows. He begged for his life, then apologized for what he had done.

"I am quite certain that the crimes of this guilty land will never be purged away but with blood. I had, as I now think, vainly flattered myself that without my bloodshed it might be done."

NAME: John Brown
YEARS OF LIFE: 1800–1859
OCCUPATION: Abolitionist

After leading a guerilla war against proslavery settlers in Kansas, John Brown put together a small force, whose purpose was to foment revolt among the slaves of the South. He chose northern Virginia as his base of operations because he hoped it would be a haven for runaway slaves who would join his "army." On October 19, 1859, Brown and his twenty-one-man army attacked, overran, and held the federal arsenal at Harper's Ferry. After a fight in which ten of his army were killed—including two of his sons—Brown was wounded and captured. As he lay in his sickbed, he said, "You may dispose of me very easily—I am nearly disposed of now—but this question is still to be settled." Brown was summarily tried and sentenced to death by hanging. This was his last written statement from his prison cell. At his execution, Ralph Waldo Emerson said, "He will make the gallows as holy as the cross."

"Where men must beg with bated breath for leave to subsist in their own land, to think their own thoughts, to sing their own songs, to garner the fruits of their own labours . . . then surely it is braver, a saner and truer thing, to be a rebel . . . than tamely to accept it as the natural lot of men."

NAME: Roger Casement
YEARS OF LIFE: 1864–1916
OCCUPATION: Irish patriot; activist

In the British consular service most of his life (and even knighted), Roger Casement was an Irish nationalist who chafed at British rule of Ireland. He experienced the humiliation of colonial rule in Ireland as a young man, but he saw colonial rule in its rawest state while in Belgian Congo, where the rubber trade and the lust for diamonds and gold engendered unfathomable brutality. He led a series of successful protests against King Leopold's rule in the Congo. After retiring from British service, Casement returned to Ireland to fight for Home Rule. He formed the Irish Volunteers, to fight with Germany against the British in World War I. He was charged with, and convicted of, high treason, and his trial—at which he uttered these words—attracted worldwide attention.

"But remember always, Dante, in the play of happiness, don't you use all for yourself only . . . help the persecuted and the victim because they are your better friends. . . . In this struggle of life you will find more and love and you will be loved."

NAME: Nicola Sacco
YEARS OF LIFE: 1891–1927
OCCUPATION: Anarchist

In 1920, in New York—during a time of great labor unrest—an anarchist named Andrea Salseda was arrested by the FBI and died in custody eight weeks later. The FBI claimed that Salseda's death was a suicide, that he had jumped from the fourteenth floor of the building. Fearing a similar fate, anarchists began carrying weapons for protection. Among these anarchists were the shoemaker Nicola Sacco and the fishmonger Bartolomeo Vanzetti, two Boston laborers and recent immigrants. They were arrested and charged with a holdup and murder, a case that was widely felt to be a frame-up. Despite flimsy evidence, they were convicted and sentenced to death by electrocution. For seven years they waited in prison, while their case became an international cause célèbre. They were both executed, amid many protests, marches, and physical confrontations with police and troops. Sacco's last words were contained in a letter to his son, Dante, written in broken English.

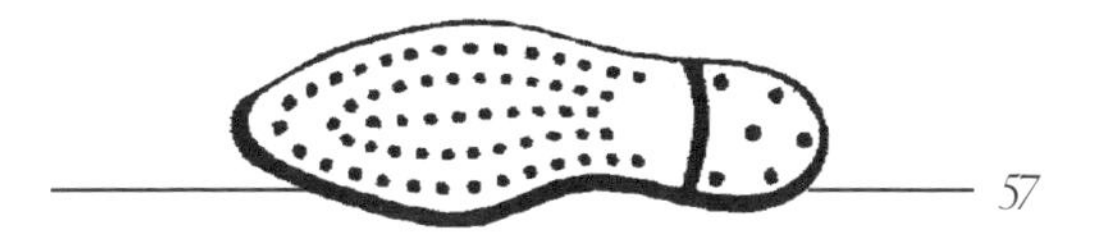

"Do not allow your conscience to trouble you in later years, not on my account. You are acting under orders, and are only doing your duty as soldiers, like myself."

NAME: Vidkun Abraham Lauritz Quisling
YEARS OF LIFE: 1887–1945
OCCUPATION: Colonel; Nazi proxy

Vidkun Quisling was Minister of Defense in Norway from 1931 to 1933, at which point he became enamored with Hitler, who had just risen to power in Germany. He started his own fascist party and established contacts with the German government. In late 1939, when it appeared the British might blockade the waters of politically neutral Norway, Quisling organized a group of sympathetic fellow officers (trained in Nazi Germany) to facilitate the invasion of his homeland by the German navy, which occurred in April 1940. With the capital, Oslo, in German hands, Quisling proclaimed himself the head of government and, via national radio, ordered all resistance to the Nazis to stop. This, however, had the opposite effect, stiffening Norwegian resistance over the next month. Quisling was "prime minister" for six days before being kicked out by the Nazis—although he was reinstated in 1942, with limited power and the utter contempt of nearly every Norwegian. At war's end, he was tried and convicted of treason, and executed on October 24, 1945. His last words were directed to the firing squad. His name is now a synonym for "traitor."

"Tell my mother I died for my country. I did what I thought was best. . . . Useless, useless."

NAME: John Wilkes Booth
YEARS OF LIFE: 1838–1865
OCCUPATION: Actor; assassin

On Good Friday, April 15, 1865, a binge-drinking actor named John Wilkes Booth, disgruntled over the recent surrender of the Confederacy, went to Ford's Theater on Tenth Street in Washington, D.C. He knew President Abraham Lincoln would be attending a performance of a popular British comedy, *Our American Cousin.* Booth knew the layout of the theater, having performed there himself. He sneaked into Lincoln's balcony box, shot him once in the back of the head with a derringer, and jumped down to the stage. Witnesses disputed what Wilkes yelled; some said "Sic semper tyrannis" (the Virginia state motto), others said "The South is avenged." Despite a broken leg, Booth managed to get on a waiting horse and elude lawmakers for twelve days; finally he was tracked to a Virginia tobacco barn. The barn was set on fire, and when Booth came out he was shot in the head. He was taken to a nearby house, where he whispered these final words.

"So that the heart be right, it is no matter which way the head lieth . . . What dost thou fear? Strike, man, strike!"

NAME: Walter Raleigh
YEARS OF LIFE: 1554–1618
OCCUPATION: Soldier; explorer; colonizer; politician; scientist

Sir Walter Raleigh's career was filled with intrigue, adventure, heroism, and scandal, and many enemies. Nonetheless, he was protected by Queen Elizabeth. When she died in 1603 and James I became king, Raleigh's fortunes waned. Accused of plotting against James, he was imprisoned, tried for conspiracy, and sentenced to death, but the sentence was not immediately carried out. Raleigh convinced James to release him in 1616, promising to secure for England a gold mine in South America. The expedition was a disaster, and upon Raleigh's return to England, the death sentence was reinstated. On the chopping block, Raleigh instructed the headsman, "When I stretch forth my hands, despatch me." He was asked to lie facing east, for "our Lord's rising"; his response is given above. The headsman finally "despatched" Raleigh with two whacks. Raleigh's head was embalmed for his widow, who kept it for twenty-nine years; it was buried with her.

"There will come a time when our silence will be more powerful than the voices you strangle today!"

"Hurrah for anarchy—this is the happiest moment of my life!"

"Hurrah for anarchy!"

"Will I be allowed to speak, O men of America? Let me speak, Sheriff Matson! Let the voice of the people be heard!"

NAMES: August Spies, Adolph Fischer, George Engel, Albert Parsons (respectively)
OCCUPATION: Anarchists

The 1880s saw much labor unrest in the United States, especially among railroad workers. The greatest railroad terminus was in Chicago, and its well-organized workers were also armed. On May 3, 1886, strikers met at the McCormick Harvester Works to stop strikebreakers from crossing the picket line. Police fired into the crowd, killing four strikers and wounding many more. On May 4, in Haymarket Square, about three thousand angry strikers met to discuss retaliation. Police ordered the meeting dispersed. Someone heaved a bomb. The police fired into the crowd. Nearly one hundred people were killed, including seven policemen. Eight union leaders (only one was actually at Haymarket Square during the riot) were arrested, tried, and convicted of "inciting murder." Labor leader Spies, Fischer, Engle, and Parsons—charged with inciting a labor riot— were executed together on November 11, 1887 in Springfield, Illinois.

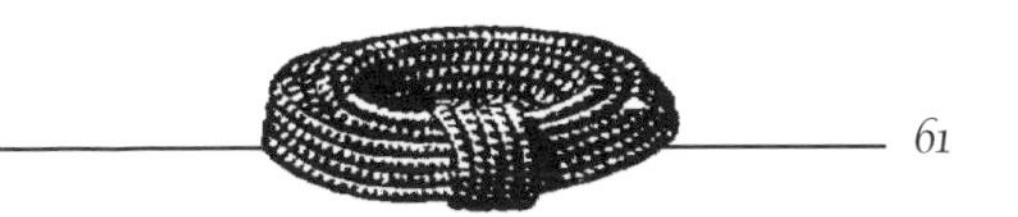

❧

"A boy has never wept, nor dashed a thousand kim. . . . Mother is the best bet and don't let Satan draw you too fast. . . . French Canadian bean soup. I want to pay George, don't make no bull moves. . . . Oh, mama, mama, mama."

NAME: Dutch Schultz (born Arthur Flegenheimer)
YEARS OF LIFE: 1902–1935
OCCUPATION: Mobster

The notorious organized crime lord Dutch Schultz was gunned down in the Palace Chop House in Newark, New Jersey, by Charlie (The Bug) Workman, an operative of rival crime lord Charles (Lucky) Luciano. Luciano had been tipped off that Schultz was planning to assassinate Thomas E. Dewey, New York's fearsome special prosecutor of organized crime. Allegedly fearing that such a killing would bring down unusual heat on the various factions of the mob (more likely, he wanted Schultz's rackets for himself), Luciano sent two gunmen to whack his rival. Shot in the head, Schultz fell face down on the tabletop. He lingered for twenty-two hours, blabbering surreal non sequiturs.

Chapter Three

On the Job

"I don't need bodyguards."

NAME: James (Jimmy) Riddle Hoffa
YEARS OF LIFE: 1913–?
OCCUPATION: Union officer

By the time Jimmy Hoffa completed his tenure as its president, the Teamsters Union was the largest labor organization in the United States. It may also have been the most corrupt, most Mafia-infiltrated, and most investigated union. After numerous congressional hearings and court appearances (including legendary showdowns with U.S. Attorney General Robert Kennedy), Hoffa went to prison in 1967, sentenced to thirteen years for jury tampering, fraud, and conspiracy. President Nixon commuted Hoffa's sentence in 1971, with the stipulation that he step down as Teamsters president and not engage in union activity. It was widely known that Hoffa did not adhere to this agreement, as he boasted in a June 1975 interview with *Playboy*. In this same interview, he scornfully deflected any suggestion that his life might be in danger. One month later, on July 30, 1975, Hoffa disappeared outside a restaurant in Bloomfield Hills, Michigan, never to be seen again.

"Let's go on to Chicago and win there."

NAME: Robert F. Kennedy
YEARS OF LIFE: 1925–1968
OCCUPATION: Attorney general of the United States; presidential candidate

After winning the momentum-shifting California Democratic primary, Robert F. Kennedy seemed well on his way to securing his party's nomination at its upcoming convention in Chicago. As he completed his victory speech to supporters at the Intercontinental Hotel in Los Angeles—a speech that ended with these words—Kennedy stepped down from the podium, crossed the banquet hall toward the hotel's kitchen, and was shot and killed by a busboy named Sirhan Sirhan, who had a score about the Middle East to settle with someone—anyone. Kennedy's death scene, like his older brother's, was broadcast live on televisions across the nation. Coming on the heels of the devastating Tet offensive in Vietnam and the assassination of Martin Luther King Jr. in Memphis, Robert Kennedy's death was almost a famous last word for the 1960s. The Democratic Party nominated Hubert Humphrey in 1968, the Chicago convention turned into a bloody battleground, and Richard Nixon won the presidential election in November.

"I may not get there with you. But I want you to know tonight that we, as a people, will get to the promised land."

NAME: Martin Luther King Jr.
YEARS OF LIFE: 1929–1968
OCCUPATION: Minister; writer; civil rights activist

The night before his assassination on April 3, 1968, Dr. King closed a speech to striking sanitation workers in Memphis, Tennessee, with these ringing and sadly prophetic words. In the months just before his death, he had expanded his vision of civil disobedience to include a protest of the Vietnam War. At the same time, FBI surveillance of his private life and political activities and threats against King and his family had increased, giving his public pronouncements an air of fatalism and foreboding. This invocation of a "promised land" recalls the majestic speech he gave at the Lincoln Memorial in Washington, D.C., in August 1963: "I have a dream that one day on the red hills of Georgia . . ."

"Brothers and sisters, stay cool!"

NAME: Malcolm X
YEARS OF LIFE: 1925–1965
OCCUPATION: Political organizer; preacher

He was born Malcolm Little, the son of a Baptist preacher who was a proponent of Marcus Garvey's black liberationist ideas and who, like Malcolm, was the victim of an assassin's bullet: Little's father was gunned down by a Ku Klux Klan-inspired group. After his father's death, Malcolm fell into the criminal life in Detroit and later in Boston; he spent time in prison for burglary but there found salvation through Elijah Muhammad's Nation of Islam. An impressive and disciplined member of the Nation, he was named minister of Temple No. 7 in Harlem. Using this forum, he became a formidable organizer and speaker. He drifted from Elijah Muhammad for various reasons, not the least of which were the latter's divisive racist views and dubious lifestyle. After a trip to Mecca, Malcolm converted to orthodox Islam and started the Organization of Afro-American Unity. He was shot and killed by rival Nation of Islam gunmen at one of his meetings, on February 21, 1965. A brave man, Malcolm X remained at the podium as the assassins ran forward with their guns, scattering chairs and terrifying the audience. As the first gunshots were fired at him, he tried to maintain order in the assembly hall, even as the bullets tore into him.

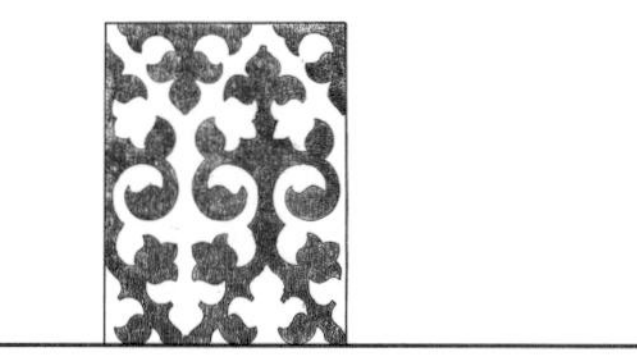

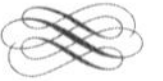

"A shilly-shally thing of milk and water, which could not last."

NAME: Alexander Hamilton
YEARS OF LIFE: 1755–1804
OCCUPATION: Delegate to the Federal Convention of 1787

As an aide-de-camp to General George Washington, Alexander Hamilton was a driving force in the American Revolution. But his political career thereafter was marked by bitter rivalries with Thomas Jefferson, James Madison, and John Adams. Hamilton, a Federalist and a hothead, believed unbendingly in tight fiscal responsibility. As secretary of the treasury, he brought order to the federal budget and created the First Bank of the United States, but he was terribly critical of the U.S. Constitution, which had just been ratified when he made the above statement in 1787. Two centuries later and counting, the Constitution has proven to be fairly sturdy. Hamilton, on the other hand, died in 1804. Unbending to the end, he was killed in a duel by Aaron Burr.

"You won't have Nixon to kick around anymore, because, gentlemen, this is my last press conference."

NAME: Richard Milhous Nixon
YEARS OF LIFE: 1913–1994
OCCUPATION: President of the United States; failed gubernatorial candidate

After losing the California gubernatorial race to Pat Brown, Richard Nixon held a press conference on November 7, 1962. Completely in character, the paranoid and self-pitying Nixon—who had done his share of ruining people's lives and careers during the Communist witch-hunts of the 1950s—vented his spleen at the reporters, whom he credited with trying to destroy him. If only he had been true to his word. Instead, Nixon worked as a corporate lawyer while slowly rebuilding a political base. Six years later, during the presidential campaign of 1968, the press had Nixon to kick around once more. Ultimately, as a result of dogged media attention to the Watergate burglary of 1972, the press kicked Nixon out of the White House.

"For the second time in our history, a British Prime Minister has returned from Germany bringing peace with honour. I believe it is peace for our time. Go home and get a nice quiet sleep."

NAME: Neville Chamberlain
YEARS OF LIFE: 1869–1940
OCCUPATION: Prime minister

On his return from Munich, where he had signed an "accord" with German dictator Adolf Hitler—which was later immortalized as an "appeasement"—Prime Minister Chamberlain addressed the nation from the steps of 10 Downing Street, on September 30, 1938. Chamberlain's desire for a peaceful settlement with the saber-rattling Hitler was not, as it has been portrayed, an act of cowardice. He realized that Great Britain was ill prepared for war, and the populace—up until this "Munich crisis"—was isolationist and relatively complacent about the troubling specter of fascism. Chamberlain's pact with Hitler was indeed an appeasement, but a calculated gamble, too, and it was also signed by the French. Unfortunately, Hitler was a better gambler, or card shark. In March 1939, in two successive weeks, he invaded Czechoslovakia and Poland. France and Great Britain were drawn into a war.

"I want to play my last game in the NBA in the nude . . . I know I won't be able to play the whole game naked, but I might be able to work something out."

NAME: Dennis Rodman
YEARS OF LIFE: Born 1963
OCCUPATION: Basketball player

One of the greatest rebounders in professional basketball history and an integral part of the Chicago Bulls' championship success, Rodman fascinated, frustrated, and angered fans throughout his tempestuous career. An intelligent, articulate, often disarmingly honest man, he is also beset with irrational, and at times self-destructive, behavior. For some time after he made this remark—reiterated in his best-selling 1996 book, *Bad As I Wanna Be*—NBA officials feared he might try to act on this impulse to disrobe in front of a capacity crowd. He never did disrobe in front of an NBA crowd. He did, however, take up professional wrestling after leaving professional basketball.

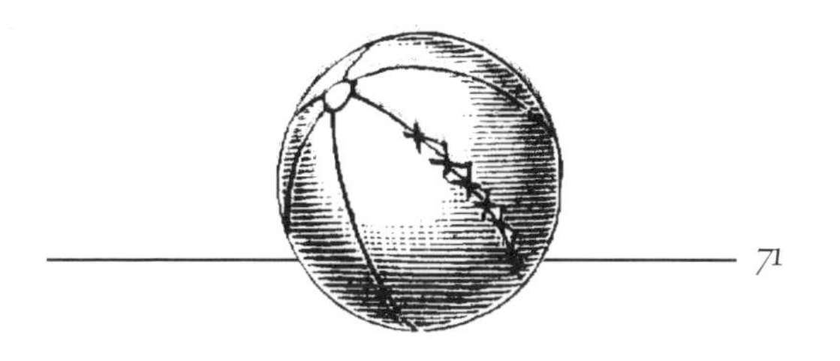

"I do not feel obliged to believe that that same God who has endowed us with sense, reason, and intellect has intended us to forgo their use."

NAME: Galileo Galilei
YEARS OF LIFE: 1564–1642
OCCUPATION: Astronomer; physicist; mathematician

About Galileo, Will Durant wrote, "No man since Archimedes had done so much for physics." Nonetheless, Galileo is best known for his contributions to astronomy, including constructing and perfecting his own telescope and using it to verify many of the revolutionary theories of his towering predecessor, Copernicus. His telescope was the most powerful on earth: he discovered ten times more stars in the heavens than had been previously cataloged. Insisting that philosophy had "gone to sleep in the lap of Aristotle," Galileo pushed for a renewed sense of wonder, experimentation, and open-mindedness in seventeenth-century Italy. He pushed too hard and fell into disfavor with the Inquisition. Although he would not renounce his belief in the Copernican view of the universe, he did promise submission to the Church. However, when he added this postscript to his remarks, the Vatican was further alarmed. Galileo's books were banned, and he was sent back to his villa where, after another controversy, he was made to live out his days under house arrest.

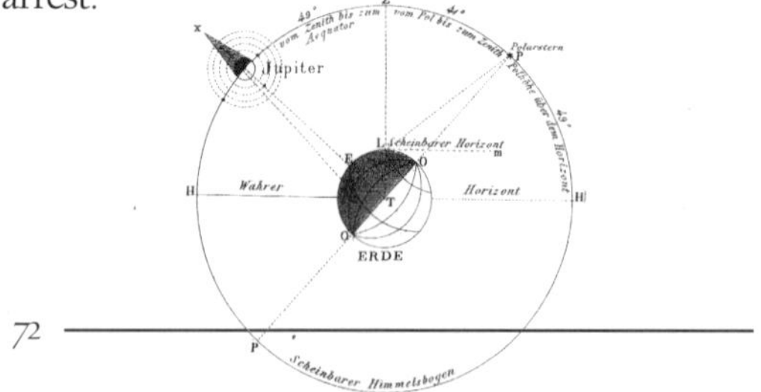

"The view that the sun stands motionless at the center of the universe is foolish, philosophically false, and utterly heretical, because contrary to Holy Scripture. The view that the earth is not the center of the universe and even has a daily rotation is philosphically false, and at least an erroneous belief."

NAME: Robert Bellarmine
YEARS OF LIFE: 1542–1621
OCCUPATION: Cardinal

With this edict from the Holy Office on March 5, 1616, Cardinal Bellarmine repudiated the work of Galileo and, for all practical purposes, ended the great astronomer-physicist's career. However, the fallout from this institutional ignorance has never faded, as the pursuit of science has continued to clash with the unwavering fundamentalism of many a religious body. This March 5 edict is often cited as one of the cornerstones of the Jeffersonian concept, later enunciated in the Enlightenment, that church and state must be separate—not only to ensure an untrammeled democracy, but to also preserve the open and fearless pursuit of knowledge, wherever it may lead.

"I have found it impossible to carry the heavy burden of responsibility and to discharge my duties as King as I would wish to do without the help and support of the woman I love."

NAME: Edward VIII
YEARS OF LIFE: 1894–1972
OCCUPATION: King

With these words, broadcast live worldwide on December 11, 1936, Edward—erstwhile Prince of Wales and, for ten months and twenty-two days, King of England—explained his abdication of the throne. The abdication had taken place just hours before in the presence of his three brothers, the Dukes of York, Gloucester, and Kent. The Duke of York immediately succeeded him to the throne; he became King George VI. Edward's live radio address was intended to "declare my allegiance to him." Indeed, the broadcast ended with Edward exclaiming, "And now we all have a new King. I wish him, and you his people, happiness and prosperity with all my heart. God bless you all! God save the King!" The "woman I love" was Mrs. Wallis Simpson, an American whose divorce did not become official until May 1937. She and Edward (now the Duke and Duchess of Windsor) were married the following month at their French chateau. They sat out World War II in Bermuda and eventually settled in Palm Beach, among other posh residences.

"I may have been given a bad break, but with all this I have a lot to live for. I consider myself the luckiest man on the face of this earth."

NAME: Henry Louis (Lou) Gehrig
YEARS OF LIFE: 1903–1941
OCCUPATION: Baseball player

On May 2, 1939, Lou Gehrig—the Iron Man, first baseman for the New York Yankees—told his manager, Joe McCarthy: "I always said that when I felt I couldn't help the team anymore, I would take myself out of the lineup. I guess that time has come." With that decision, Gehrig's amazing consecutive game streak, which stretched from June 1, 1925, to May 2, 1939 (2,130 games total), came to an end. One of the most touching moments in sports history occurred two months later, on July 4, 1939, when Yankee Stadium hosted Lou Gehrig Appreciation Day. The normally stoic Gehrig stepped to the microphone and, with tears streaming down his face, made this statement. His famed teamate, Babe Ruth, himself showing signs of physical deterioration, hugged his old teammate. Gehrig died in June 1941, of amyotrophic lateral sclerosis (now called Lou Gehrig's disease). His consecutive game streak, thought to be untouchable, was broken by Cal Ripken Jr. on September 6, 1995. Ripken went on to establish his own record of 2,632 consecutive games played.

"But I still remember the refrain of one of the most popular barrack ballads of that day, which proclaimed, most proudly, that 'Old soldiers never die. They just fade away.' And like the soldier of the ballad, I now close my military career and just fade away—an old soldier who tried to do his duty as God gave him the light to see that duty. . . . Goodbye."

NAME: Douglas MacArthur
YEARS OF LIFE: 1880–1964
OCCUPATION: Commanding general, U.S. Army, Far East

On April 12, 1951, President Harry Truman relieved General Douglas MacArthur of duty after a series of insubordinate acts and provocations. Upon his return from Korea, MacArthur addressed a joint session of the U.S. Congress. He reiterated his belief that Manchuria should be bombed and China blockaded. (In 1950 he had asked that twenty-six atomic bombs be dropped on North Korea and Red China.) His speech, carried live on U.S. television, received thirty standing ovations from Congress, but Truman characterized it as "a bunch of damn bull-shit." MacArthur didn't fade away immediately, either; he was Robert Taft's running mate in 1952 in an unsuccessful bid for the Republican presidential nomination.

"God, don't let me die. I have so much to do."

NAME: Huey Pierce Long, aka "Kingfish"
YEARS OF LIFE: 1893–1935
OCCUPATION: Governor

Huey Long ran the state of Louisiana like a tyrant—a benign dictator to the Anglo-Saxon poor, his main constituency, and a fearsome demagogue to most everyone else. Carl Weiss, a doctor whose father-in-law had lost his judgeship through maneuverings by the Kingfish, had had enough of the govenor's chicanery by September 8, 1935. On that day, he hid behind a pillar in the state capitol. When Long came out of a legislative session without his bodyguards, Weiss leaped out and shot Long in the stomach. Long shouted, "I'm shot!" as he continued to hurry down the hall. His bodyguards shot Weiss thirty-two times. Weiss's gunshot was not initially fatal, but the surgeon who operated on Long did not notice the governor's punctured kidney. Long died two days later, the realization that his political career was over coming to him in his very last breath.

"KHAQQ calling Itasca. We must be on you, but cannot see you. Gas is running low."

NAME: Amelia Earhart
YEARS OF LIFE: 1897–1937
OCCUPATION: Pilot

One of the most remarkable women in modern history, Amelia Earhart is also one of its most enduring mysteries. After gaining household-name status for her aviation feats (she was the first woman to fly solo across the Atlantic Ocean, first to fly solo from Honolulu to Oakland, first to fly nonstop from Mexico City to Newark), she wanted to make the ultimate flying trip, a circumnavigation of the globe. On the last leg of this extraordinary journey, she disappeared. This was the last message that Earhart radioed from her plane before disappearing in the South Pacific on July 2, 1937. "We" was she and navigator Fred Noonan; their silver Lockheed Electra went down somewhere between New Guinea and Howland Island. Despite a massive search by the U.S. Navy, immediately dispatched by her friend and champion President Roosevelt, no traces of plane or bodies were ever found. No definitive theory or explanation has ever been tendered. Earhart was renowned for her generosity to family, friends, and fans as well as for her stubborn loyalty to colleagues—even when it was dangerous to her personal safety. Indeed, hiring Fred Noonan, former chief navigator for Pan Am but an alleged problem drinker, for her final flight is an eloquent case in point. Earhart had survived many near crashes and crackups before her final one.

Chapter Four

On the Field of Battle

"Hurrah, boys, we've got them! We'll finish them up and then go home to our station."

NAME: George Armstrong Custer
YEARS OF LIFE: 1839–1876
OCCUPATION: General, U.S. Army

Throughout his military career, General Custer gained a reputation for headstrong, sometimes ill-advised, bravery. For his courage under fire in the Civil War, he was made a brevet brigadier general in the Union army, the youngest on record (he was twenty-three). He came to national attention during the Indian wars of the 1870s. Twice suspended from the army and deeply reviled by the native peoples of the northern plains, Custer was a disaster waiting to happen. On June 25, 1876, he led his 7th Cavalry, against orders, into the camp of Sitting Bull's Sioux and Cheyenne alliance near the Little Big Horn River. Upon sighting the Indian campfires, Custer was certain of his surprise attack's swift success—it wasn't. The result was an overwhelming victory for the beleaguered Sitting Bull. One of the Cavalry's survivors, Sergeant Windolph, reported these to be the last words he heard Custer say.

"They couldn't hit an elephant at this dist–"

NAME: John B. Sedgwick
YEARS OF LIFE: 1813–1864
OCCUPATION: Union general

General John Sedgwick was a career officer, having served with distinction in the Mexican War in the 1840s and the Indian wars in the 1850s. When the Civil War broke out, he was a lieutenant, overseeing the construction of fortresses in Colorado. He volunteered to serve in the war; quickly promoted to lieutenant colonel, colonel, and brigadier general, he commanded a division of the Army of the Potomac. Displaying uncommon bravery, Sedgwick was wounded twice in battle and promoted to major general by 1863. In May 1864, he was overseeing the emplacement of artillery near Spotsylvania, Virginia, when he was killed instantly by a Confederate sharpshooter.

"I tell you Wellington is a bad general, the English are bad soldiers; we will settle the matter by lunchtime."

NAME: Napoleon Bonaparte
YEARS OF LIFE: 1769–1821
OCCUPATION: Emperor

The charismatic Corsican Napoleon Bonaparte (born Nabulio Buonaparte) made a career out of famous last words. He compulsively and histrionically offered them to his soldiers, who hung on every word and recorded them for posterity. After a military coup in 1799 made him dictator of France, Napoleon spent the next ten years at war across Europe, compiling military successes, land grabs, and power on the scale of Alexander the Great (one of his self-conscious models). After his defeat at Leipzig in 1813, Bonaparte abdicated and went to Elba, only to return to France a year later to try to re-create his empire. This pipe dream lasted until June 18, 1815, when the combined armies of England and Germany—led by Wellington—handed Napoleon his final defeat. At breakfast on the morning of Waterloo, Napoleon offered these grandly mistaken words to his generals. While not the last he ever spoke alive, they were the last words he ever spoke from a position of power.

"Nobody can overthrow me. I have the support of 700,000 troops, all the workers, and most of the people. I have the power."

NAME: Mohammad Reza Shah Pahlavi
YEARS OF LIFE: 1919–1980
OCCUPATION: Shah

When the Shah of Iran made this statement to the *Washington Post* on March 6, 1978, he could also count on the support of President Jimmy Carter. Two months previously, Carter had offered some famous last words of his own: "Because of the greatness of the Shah, Iran is an island of stability in the Middle East." Nine months later, on January 16, 1979, the Shah was driven into exile by the continued civic strife in Iran, brought on both by popular desire to return to fundamentalist Islam and the corruption and brutality of Pahlavi's regime. The Shah sought safe haven in Egypt, Morocco, the Bahamas, and Mexico. On November 4, 1979, two weeks after he entered the United States for cancer treatment, Iranians stormed the American Embassy in Teheran; sixty-three hostages were taken and held more than a year. The Shah died before they were released.

"Order A. P. Hill to prepare for action. Pass the infantry to the front . . . Tell Major Hawks . . . Let us pass over the river and rest under the shade of the trees."

NAME: Thomas Jonathan (Stonewall) Jackson
YEARS OF LIFE: 1824–1863
OCCUPATION: Confederate general

At Chancellorsville, in northern Virginia, General Joseph Hooker was overconfident that he was poised to destroy Robert E. Lee's forces. Lee, in collaboration with Stonewall Jackson, devised a plan that would split their armies and outflank Hooker by surprise attack from the rear. It worked. Chancellorsville, which took place from May 1 to May 6, 1863, was a major Confederate victory and an embarrassment to President Lincoln, who had put Hooker in charge just before the battle. But the Confederacy suffered a terrible blow, too. During frantic nighttime maneuverings, Jackson's small party returned to its own lines, but Confederate sentries mistakenly opened fire. Two men were killed instantly, and Jackson was wounded by three bullets. His left arm was amputated, and although he rallied, he died May 10, a Sunday. "I have always desired to die on Sunday," he said, then fell asleep. He woke suddenly a few hours later and cried out these final orders, then died.

"Sopherl, Sopherl, stirb nicht . . . Bleib am Leben für unsere Kinder!" ("Little Sophie, little Sophie, don't die! . . . Stay alive for our children!")

NAME: Franz Ferdinand
YEARS OF LIFE: 1863–1914
OCCUPATION: Crown prince; nephew of Franz Joseph, Austro-Hungarian emperor

Gavrilo Princip's assassination of the archduke and putative future emperor Franz Ferdinand in Sarajevo is generally regarded as a precipitating event of World War I. Princip, a Bosnian student, was part of a fanatical group called the Black Hand, which plotted to end Hapsburg Dynasty rule and reestablish a Serbian monarchy. He and his cronies staked out the archduke's parade route and waited alongside the boulevard with homemade bombs, Browning pistols, and capsules of cyanide (so as not to be taken alive). Because the crowd was too thick for the bomb to be thrown, Princip stepped up to the car and fired two shots, each proving fatal. The archduke was struck in the jugular and the duchess Sophie Chotek in the abdomen. Both bled to death in the car before medical help could provide any hope for survival.

"What animal is that which in the morning goes on four feet, at noon on two, and in the evening upon three?"

NAME: The Sphinx
OCCUPATION: Monster in Thebes

According to Greek mythology, not long after Oedipus unwittingly murdered his father Laius, King of Thebes, the area was tormented by a monster that crept in among the rocks on the main road beyond the city limits. This monster, known as the Sphinx, had the body of a lion and the head of a woman. All passersby were required to answer its riddle. Those who answered correctly were allowed to pass; those who botched it were killed. No one, until Oedipus, had answered it correctly. He sauntered out and, hearing the riddle proposed by the Sphinx, answered, "Man, who in childhood creeps on hands and knees, in manhood walks erect, and in old age with the aid of a staff." Distraught that her riddle had been solved, the Sphinx dashed herself upon the rocks and died. Thebes showed its gratitude to Oedipus by making him king and giving him Queen Jocasta's hand in marriage. Thus in ignorance he married his mother.

"I charge you to keep at a moderate height, for if you fly too low the damp will clog your wings, and if too high the heat will melt them. Keep near me and you will be safe."

NAME: Daedelus
OCCUPATION: Inventor; architect

In Greek mythology, Daedelus was a mechanical genius who won the favor of King Minos for constructing the elaborate labyrinth in which the king had trapped Theseus. Daedelus got on Minos's wrong side, however, and found himself under arrest. Because the king kept vigilant naval and ground forces, Daedelus set about making a set of wings for himself and for his son. "Minos may control the land and sea, but not the regions of the air. I will try that way," said Daedelus. He bound his own large, cumbersome set of wings with thread, but he used wax to bind the feathers on the smaller pair for his son, Icarus. Just before takeoff, Daedelus offered these parting words to his son. These are the last words Icarus heard. He disobeyed his father and flew too close to the sun; the wax melted and his wings came apart. He plunged to his death in the sea off Sicily.

"Give them the cold steel, boys."

NAME: Lewis Armistead
YEARS OF LIFE: 1817–1863
OCCUPATION: Confederate general

The third day of the Battle of Gettysburg, July 3, 1863, started with a bloody exchange of artillery shells. The Confederate forces, commanded personally by General Lee, intended to soften the Union lines to prepare for a charge of thirteen thousand men led by General George E. Pickett. The charge resulted in a slaughter of the Confederates, and the only breech in the Union lines was at a place called the Angle, where a bend in the stone wall behind which the forces were massed allowed some penetration. The Confederate forces at this point were led by General Lewis A. Armistead. Just before leaping over the wall, waving his hat on the point of his sword, Armistead yelled these words to his men. He was shot down after commandeering a Union battery. Before he died, he handed his personal effects to Union General Winfield Scott Hancock, a friend from before the war, to be sent back to his family in North Carolina.

"And take care of my dear Lady Hamilton, Hardy, take care of poor Lady Hamilton. Kiss me, Hardy . . . Remember that I leave Lady Hamilton and my daughter Horatia as a legacy to my country. Thank God I have done my duty."

NAME: Horatio Nelson
YEARS OF LIFE: 1758–1805
OCCUPATION: Admiral

The naval battle at Trafalgar on October 21, 1805, was an intense struggle between the British fleet, commanded by Admiral Horatio Nelson—a national icon in England; the Hero of the Nile (a bloody nighttime naval engagement that finished Napoleon's ambitions in Egypt)—and the combined forces of France and Spain. In the heat of the action, Nelson's command ship, HMS *Victory*, pulled alongside the French ship *Temeraire*, drawing intense gunfire from both sides. As Nelson and Captain Thomas Masterman Hardy paced the deck, Hardy's shoe buckle was shot off. Within minutes Nelson was shot at close quarters and carried into the cockpit, to the ship's surgeon, William Beatty, who gave the fullest account of Nelson's death. Nelson died content in the knowledge that the enemy fleet had been defeated.

"Don't give up the ship."

Name: James Lawrence
Years of Life: 1781–1813
Occupation: Captain, U.S. Navy

The War of 1812 (which actually lasted from 1812 to 1815) has rightly been called the Second War of Independence. Britain, embroiled in a lengthy war with France, had begun blockading European ports to keep supplies from reaching their enemies. This action of course sharply reduced American exports. Furthermore, British naval vessels were stopping American ships on the high seas and press-ganging their crews into military service. Britain's distinct edge (the world's strongest navy) was dulled in 1812 and 1813, when smaller American vessels proved a formidable match for the British frigates. One of the most famous naval battles was fought on June 1, 1813, between the frigate HMS *Shannon* and the USS *Chesapeake,* under the command of Captain James Lawrence. After a hard-fought battle in which Lawrence was mortally wounded, the *Shannon* captured the *Chesapeake.* But it was a Pyrrhic victory, as the courage the captain and his crew displayed, exemplified in Lawrence's last words, were put about to buoy the ultimately successful American war efforts over the next two years.

Chapter Five

On Stage

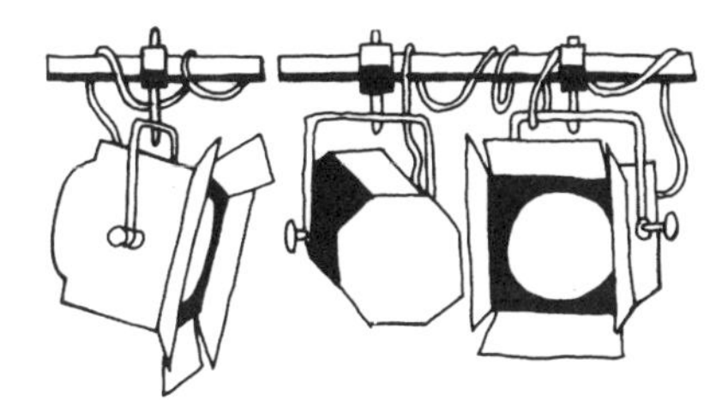

"I kiss'd thee ere I kill'd thee:
no way but this,
Killing myself to die upon a kiss."

NAME: Othello
PLAY: *Othello*, Act V, scene II
OCCUPATION: Military hero
AUTHOR: William Shakespeare (1564–1616)

Othello's is one of the most heartrending death scenes in literature. Not only has the noble Moor Othello realized the scope of the deception rendered him by Iago, but he begs those he has wronged—most pointedly, Cassio—to not speak of "these unlucky deeds" with malice in their hearts. At worst, he feels he deserves the title "honourable murderer"—"for naught I did in hate, but all in honour"—and, at best, his sin was having "loved not wisely, but too well." Othello does at least get one stab at Iago before his sword is taken away from him. The wounded Iago, whom Othello now calls "a demi-devil," vows that "from this time forth, I shall not speak." Surrounding these two are their dead wives—Emilia, whom Iago has killed for revealing his deception, and Desdemona, upon whom Othello falls after stabbing himself with "a sword of Spain, the ice brook's temper," which he has concealed from the others. Cassio proclaims Othello to be "great of heart."

"A horse! a horse! my kingdom for a horse!"

NAME: Richard III
PLAY: *King Richard III,* Act V, scene IV
OCCUPATION: King of England, 1483–1485
AUTHOR: William Shakespeare (1564–1616)

Although Shakespeare was correct in *King Richard III*—depicting the horseless king's death in battle—the sketchy historical record has Richard actually saying, "I will die King of England! I will not budge a foot! Treason! Treason!" While technically incorrect, Shakespeare was true to the spirit of that day on the fields of Bosworth, and his version of Richard's famous last words are assumed by most to be the truth. In the play, Richard is killed by Richmond, who announces, "The day is ours, the bloody dog is dead." While no record exists to verify whether this event took place, it is true that Richard's dead body was unceremoniously tied to a horse and buried without honor in the church of the Greyfriars. For dramatic effect, Shakespeare exaggerated Richard's physical and mental deformities. In truth, he was not a hunchback and was only a bit more Machiavellian than most rulers of his day, and his reign as king of England was brief.

"Here's to my love! O true apothecary,
Thy drugs are quick. Thus with a kiss I die."

NAME: Romeo
PLAY: *Romeo and Juliet,* Act V, scene III
OCCUPATION: Son to Montague
AUTHOR: William Shakespeare (1564–1616)

The romance of Romeo and Juliet is doomed from the start: they are members of two Verona clans, or "houses"—the Montagues and Capulets, respectively—that are embroiled in a blood feud. The backdrop of bitter enmity makes the romance between the two young lovers deeper, sweeter, and ultimately more tragic. They have agreed to wed in secrecy, against their families' wishes. Their plans are discovered and Capulet forbids the marriage, arranging instead that Juliet marry Paris, kinsman to the Prince of Verona. Rather than go through with the wedding, Juliet poisons herself (her last words: "Romeo, Romeo, Romeo! Here's drink—I drink to thee"). When Romeo learns of her death, he purchases a dram of poison and goes to Juliet's grave, where he finds Paris. They fight and Romeo kills Paris, then takes the poison and falls dead on Juliet's grave. The final words cited here are actually the last two lines of a forty-five-line soliloquy. The play itself possesses some famous last words, too: "For never was a story of more woe / Than this of Juliet and her Romeo."

"O town of my fathers in Thebes' land.
O gods of our house
I am led away at last.
Look, leaders of Thebes,
I am the last of your royal line.
Look what I suffer, at whose command,
because I respected the right."

NAME: Antigone
PLAY: *Antigone*
OCCUPATION: Daughter of Oedipus and Jocasta
AUTHOR: Sophocles (c.496–406 B.C.)

After Oedipus discovers his horrible mistake—he has killed his father, Laius, and married his mother, Jocasta—he goes mad and puts out his eyes, wandering blindly out of Thebes. Antigone accompanies her father during his last days. After he dies, she famously laments, "Alas! I only wished I might have died with my poor father: wherefore should I ask for a longer life?" But she does have a longer life, filled with woe. Her brothers—Eteocles and Polynices—vying for control of Thebes after their father's banishment, kill each other in a duel. Eteocles is buried with honor; Polynices is left to rot where he has fallen. In violation of the new king's order, Antigone tries to bury her brother, but she is caught and ordered buried alive.

"O Holy mother mine,
O Sky that circling brings the light to all,
you see me, how I suffer, how unjustly."

NAME: Prometheus
PLAY: *Prometheus*
OCCUPATION: Titan
AUTHOR: Aeschylus (525–456 B.C.)

Prometheus, according to Greek myth and legend, was the greatest friend and benefactor humankind ever had. He and his Titan brother Epimetheus had been given the tasks of making mankind and of providing all the animals of creation the means by which they might survive and prosper. With the aid of Minerva, Prometheus stole fire from the chariot of the sun and brought it down to Earth, concealed in a hollow fennel stalk, to give to man. With fire, man could make weapons and tools, stay warm, and mint coins. For his theft of fire, Prometheus was chained to a desolate mountainside. He still had not learned the lesson that Hermes wanted to drive home at the end of the play: "When you are trapped by ruin, don't blame fortune: / Don't say that Zeus has brought you to calamity / That you could not foresee . . . but blame yourselves."

"Yes, that's what you hope, Judge, isn't it? Now that you are cock-of-the-walk."

NAME: Hedda Gabler
PLAY: *Hedda Gabler* (1890)
OCCUPATION: Frustrated housewife
AUTHOR: Henrik Ibsen (1828–1906)

Hedda Gabler is married to Jorgen Tesman, a "holder of a scholarship for research in the History of Civilization" and an ambitious academic toady. But she loves Eljert Lovborg, a dissipated scholar and visionary, who represents the individual freedom and impulsive behavior for which she longs. Hedda acts out her longing for freedom by flaunting her prowess at pistol shooting and by banging out wild dance music on a piano. After Lovberg is shot to death with one of her pistols, the oppressive burden of her life as a housewife to a wholly unemotional man becomes more than she can bear. Judge Brack, a lubricious family friend, tries to console Hedda by offering to keep company with her while her scholarly husband labors over his studies: "I'm sure we'll have a very jolly time together, we two." From offstage, "in a loud, clear voice," Hedda offers these famous last words just before "a shot is heard within." Her clueless husband observes: "Now she is playing with those pistols again." In fact, she is dead from a self-inflicted bullet wound. *Hedda Gabler* was a groundbreaking role for women in modern theater.

"Whoever you are—I have always depended on the kindness of strangers."

NAME: Blanche DuBois
PLAY: *A Streetcar Named Desire* (1947)
OCCUPATION: Houseguest; sister of Stella Kowalski
AUTHOR: Tennessee Williams (1911–1983)

When Blanche DuBois arrives at her sister Stella's apartment in New Orleans, she has no money or prospects. But she has concocted a fantasy about an old suitor named Shep Huntleigh, who will come to her rescue. She proceeds to drive Stella's husband, Stanley, as mad as she is. Filled with rage at her lies, putdowns, and disruption of his domestic life, Stanley rapes Blanche. Unable to believe Blanche's story about the rape, Stella (just returned from the hospital with a baby) arranges to have Blanche committed to a state mental institution. Now completely delusional, Blanche has convinced herself that it is Shep Huntleigh who is coming for her; when the doctor appears, she says, "You are not the gentleman I was expecting." After retreating and resisting, Blanche finally agrees to go quietly with the doctor. She "extends her hands toward the Doctor," and "holding tight to his arm," she walks out the door as she makes this parting statement, one of the most famous in American theater history.

"Adieu, mes amis. Je vais la gloire." ("Farewell, my friends. I go to glory.")

NAME: Isadora Duncan
YEARS OF LIFE: 1877–1927
OCCUPATION: Dancer

The flamboyant American dancer Angela (Isadora) Duncan was noted as much for her revolutionary choreography—which emphasized natural movements rather than technical precision—as for her radical politics and wide-open lifestyle. She had two children by two different men—both out of wedlock and both drowned in a 1913 car accident. By the end of her life, Duncan was living "precariously" in Nice, on the French Riviera. Typical of her flair for the dramatic—possibly prophetic, too—was this histrionic good-bye to friends, delivered as if from stage, as she climbed into the back of a car on September 14, 1927. Her long scarf became entangled in one of the limousine's wheels, and before the driver could stop the vehicle, she had been strangled.

“Ever get the feeling you’ve been cheated?”

NAME: Johnny Rotten (born John Lydon)
YEARS OF LIFE: Born 1956
OCCUPATION: Musician; anarchist

Lydon called this pronouncement “my famous last words on stage.” It was the valedictory statement of his incarnation as Johnny Rotten, singer for the anarchic Sex Pistols. The date was September 14, 1978, and the place was Winterland, a cavernous music hall in San Francisco. The concert was the last stop on the band’s manic tour of the United States. Earlier in the day, the band’s ill-fated bass player, Sid Vicious, had scored some heroin three weeks after Rotten (his best, and perhaps, only friend) had managed to keep him off hard drugs. The other band members had stopped speaking to Rotten; the manager hadn’t booked him a motel room. Reflecting on the meteoric rise and fall of his band, Lydon wrote, in *Rotten* (1994), “The Sex Pistols ended the way they began—in utter disaster. Everything between was equally disastrous.” Despite that, the preternaturally cynical Lydon admitted, “It was vile. Really, really bad, but I liked it.”

"Hope I die before I get old."

NAME: Peter Townshend
YEARS OF LIFE: Born 1945
OCCUPATION: Rock musician; writer

Sung by Roger Daltry of The Who, and written by Peter Townshend, the band's windmill-style guitarist, this line from the song "My Generation" is one of the most famous in rock 'n' roll history. Not necessarily a suicide note or a death wish, this line perfectly encapsulates the live-fast,-die-young,-leave-a-beautiful-corpse philosophy that underscored the "rock revolution" of the 1960s and very much described The Who's destructive stage antics at the peak of their skills. Although Townshend and Daltry did not take the lyrics to heart—both still very much alive—the band's drummer, Keith Moon, seemed to embody the live-for-today spirit, dying in 1978 of an accidental drug overdose. Years later, another band (They Might Be Giants) turned The Who's line on its head, with "I hope that I get old before I die."

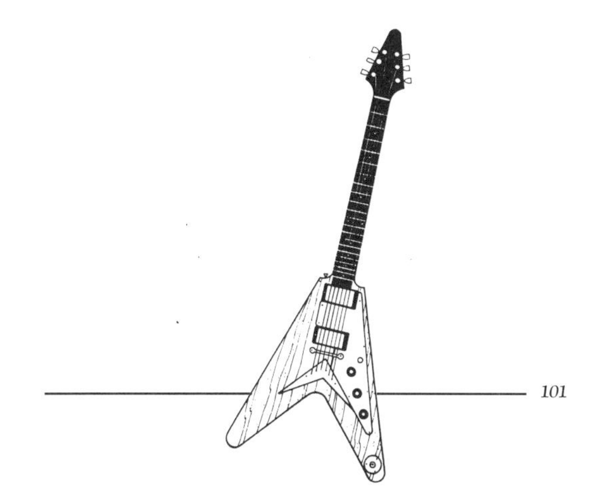

"On the whole, I'd rather be in Philadelphia."

NAME: William Claude (W. C.) Fields
YEARS OF LIFE: 1880–1946
OCCUPATION: Comedian; juggler

One of the ongoing shticks of W. C. Fields's brilliant career in comedy was his denigration of the City of Brotherly Love. This geographical gaffe became so linked with him that it has, apocryphally, been deemed his epitaph, and allegedly his last words. Because Fields was cremated, not buried, this cannot be verified (the words do not appear on the vault where his ashes are stashed). Nonetheless, he was fond of the expression, although he originally "borrowed" it from *Vanity Fair,* which had used it as a punch line for a joke. Bygones must have been bygones, because in 1925, Fields sent *Vanity Fair* a variation for an article on the tombstone inscriptions of famous people. (Dorothy Parker's were "Excuse My Dust.")

"Oh, you young people act like old men. You are no fun."

NAME: Josephine Baker
YEARS OF LIFE: 1906–1975
OCCUPATION: Singer; dancer

Josephine Baker lived her life on her own terms. She fled childhood poverty in St. Louis, running away from home as a teenager to join a traveling vaudeville company. Tired of the cartoonish roles and limited mobility offered African Americans in entertainment, she moved to Paris and achieved international superstardom in the 1920s. Bored with the usual stage conceits, she danced bare-breasted, made outrageous stage entrances, and wore flamboyant costumes. Disgusted with America's slowness to integrate, she demanded service for all comers in any club or concert hall where she played. Baker spoke her final words in Paris to a young man who had brought her back to her apartment when she wanted to stay out late. She died in her sleep, of a massive stroke, that same night.

"'Well? Shall we go?'
'Yes, let's go.'
They do not move."

NAMES: Estragon and Vladimir
PLAY: *Waiting for Godot* (1954)
OCCUPATION: Bums
AUTHOR: Samuel Beckett (1906–1989)

Like "a sharp stab of beauty and pain," Samuel Beckett's *Waiting for Godot* altered the course of world theater when it appeared in 1954. The tale of two desperate but paralyzed seekers—of help, religion, comfort, anything—*Waiting for Godot* perfectly captured postwar anxieties and brought instant recognition to an inscrutable Irish author, then nearing fifty years of age. The plight of the hapless Estragon and Vladimir—whose speeches here are the play's final exchange, followed by the final stage direction—has become a staple of theater troupes around the world. Beckett subtitled the play "a tragicomedy in two acts."

Chapter Six

On the Screen

"Louie, I think this is the beginning of a beautiful friendship."

NAME: Rick
MOVIE: *Casablanca* (1942)
OCCUPATION: Club and casino proprietor

In this famous last line from *Casablanca,* Rick (played by Humphrey Bogart) is speaking to French police captain Louie Renault (Claude Rains) after the latter has turned a convenient blind eye to his plans to help his ex-lover, Ilsa Lund Laszlo (Ingrid Bergman), and her husband, freedom fighter Victor Laszlo (Paul Henreid), escape to America. Gestapo agents track the Laszlos to Casablanca, a seaport in the French colony of Morocco, where the world-weary Rick operates Café Americain. After much soul-searching and booze—and despite Ilsa's jilting him in Paris a few years earlier—Rick sticks his neck out for the Laszlos, with Louie's tacit help. This heroic act is out of character for both men. Rick and Louie, although often at odds over legal matters, are cut from the same pragmatic survivor's cloth. At the end, they walk off together in the fog, having agreed to leave Casablanca for Brazzaville until the whole thing blows over. In real life, Bogart's last words—according to his wife Lauren Bacall—were "Goodbye, Kid. Hurry back."

"Rosebud."

NAME: Charles Foster Kane
MOVIE: *Citizen Kane* (1941)
OCCUPATION: Newspaper mogul

For his big screen debut, director Orson Welles wrote the screenplay and starred in the lead role of *Citizen Kane,* a thinly veiled, grandly expressionist, fictionalized life of newspaper baron William Randolph Hearst (1863–1951). The film begins at the end, with the now-pathetic Kane on his deathbed inside Xanadu, the forbidding Florida palace he has filled with baubles and bibelots—evidence of his unfathomable wealth. Gripping a crystal glass ball filled with fake snow, Kane expires; his last whispered word is "Rosebud." The rest of the film is an attempt to ascertain what this inscrutable utterance meant. The journalist assigned to ferret it out concludes, "I guess Rosebud is just a piece in a jigsaw puzzle—a missing piece." But perceptive viewers will make their own guesses. Hearst threatened to sue Welles over the unflattering portrait, but he limited his revenge to barring ads for the film in his newspapers. Welles had the last word: *Citizen Kane* is now regarded as one of the finest motion pictures ever made.

"What have I done?"

NAME: Colonel Nicholson
MOVIE: *The Bridge on the River Kwai* (1957)
OCCUPATION: British leader in Japanese P.O.W. camp

The British Colonel Nicholson (played by Alec Guiness) has been captured, along with his men, by the Japanese and placed in a jungle prison camp in Burma. (The film was shot mostly in Ceylon.) He is a model of discipline and rectitude, refusing, at his own physical cost, to let his men be mistreated. Nicholson rallies the prisoners to help in the construction of a railroad bridge across the River Kwai, connecting the Japanese supply lines and helping their war effort. In the process of completing this remarkable feat of ad hoc engineering, he comes to see the bridge as his personal creation. When he discovers that the bridge has been mined, he panics and tries to stop the sabotage, although it was done by an Allied guerrilla team. After having caused the death of some of the Allies, Nicholson realizes the delusion under which he has suffered. He barks out this question, then lurches toward the detonating device and collapses, dead, on its handle. The bridge is blown. The train tumbles into the gorge. Surveying the carnage, Major Clipton, the camp doctor, utters the famous last words in the film: "Madness! Madness!"

"You cursed brat. Look what you've done. I'm melting . . . melting. O what a world! What a world! Who would have thought a good little girl like you could destroy my beautiful wickedness."

NAME: Wicked Witch of the West
MOVIE: *The Wizard of Oz* (1939)
OCCUPATION: Wicked witch

Upon being transported by a Kansas tornado to the Land of Oz, Dorothy crosses paths with the Wicked Witch of the West (Margaret Hamilton), who bears an uncanny resemblance to her nasty real-life neighbor, Elmira Gulch. Because Dorothy's house has fallen upon "Elmira's" sister witch, the Wicked Witch vows revenge; for the rest of the film, as Dororthy and her companions make their way toward the Emerald City, the Witch of the West haunts their every move. She finally catches up with Dorothy on the outskirts of the Emerald City. In a fit of rage, she sets fire to the Scarecrow. Dorothy retrieves a bucket of water and throws it on her faithful friend, but some of the water sloshes onto the Wicked Witch, who proceeds to melt away before their eyes. The witch's famous last words in the film bear only a passing resemblance to the ones from the original 1900 book, *The Wonderful Wizard of Oz*, by L. Frank Baum.

"Shoot straight, you bastards! Don't make a mess of it!"

NAME: Harry Harbord (Breaker) Morant
MOVIE: *Breaker Morant* (1979)
OCCUPATION: Lieutenant in the British-led Bushveldt Carbineers; poet

All the events depicted in this stunning courtroom drama were true. In November 1901, at the peak of hostilities in the Boer War, three Australian soldiers were made scapegoats by the British Army after a number of Boer (Dutch) prisoners and a German missionary were shot in retaliation for the mutilation of a British officer. Considered "colonials," the Aussies were expendable; their convictions were meant to assuage the German government, even though the trio had verbal orders from Lord Kitchener to shoot prisoners. Lieutenant Morant (played by Edward Woodward in the movie) was a gifted poet and a renowned horse trainer (breaker)—"the best in Australia." When in the film he and Lieutenant Peter Hancock walked, hand in hand, to their position in front of the firing squad, he says, "Well, Peter, this is what comes of empire building". Just moments earlier, he had handed his lawyer a poem, and said, "See that this gets published, will you? We poets do crave immortality, you know."

"You know, those clowns outside are going to give me a pretty good going over, for the codes. I don't know how well I could stand up under torture . . . Well, Mandrake, I happen to believe in a life after this one. And I know I'll have to answer for what I've done. And I think I can."

NAME: General Jack D. Ripper
MOVIE: *Dr. Strangelove, or How I Learned to Stop Worrying and Love the Bomb* (1964)
OCCUPATION: Air Force base commander

Ripper (Sterling Hayden), paranoid over "Commies," activates emergency war strategy Plan R, sending over thirty U.S. bombers, each with a nuclear device, to hit targets inside the Soviet Union. Only he knows the codes that can recall the planes. Captain Mandrake (Peter Sellers) plays along with Ripper's psychotic ramblings, hoping he will somehow spill the codes' essence, thus averting the destruction of life on Earth. After uttering the above words, Ripper enters the bathroom; moments later, a pistol shot is heard. The good news: Mandrake pieces together the recall code from Ripper's repeated words "purity of essence" (POE). The bad news: it doesn't matter.

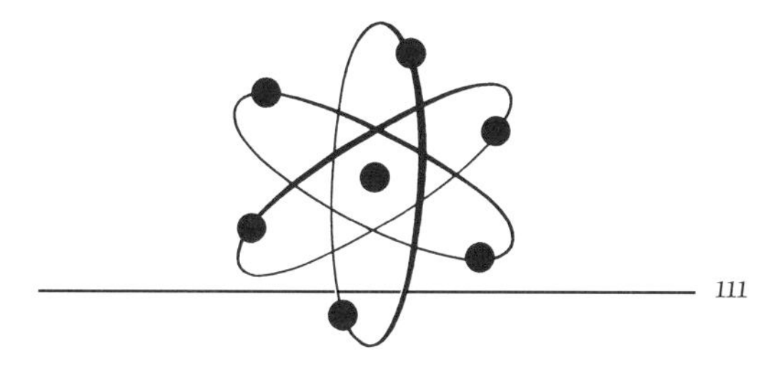

"He wasn't a bad fellow. No worse than most and probably better than some. And not a bad ballplayer neither, when they gave him a chance, when they laid off him long enough. From here on in I rag nobody."

NAME: Henry Wiggin
FILM: *Bang the Drum Slowly* (1973)
OCCUPATION: Major league pitcher

Before spring training, Bruce Pearson, third-string catcher for the New York Mammoths, learns he has contracted a fatal disease. The only one who knows about it is star pitcher Henry Wiggin (played by Michael Moriarty). Pearson, played with naïve charm by Robert De Niro, is a dim hayseed from Georgia, the butt of many jokes in the club. "He was almost too dumb to play a joke on, and now he'd had the biggest joke of all played on him," says Wiggin, who takes it upon himself to serve as Pearson's guardian angel. Pearson's take on death: "I been handed a shit deal. I'm doomeded." Rather than play it as a soap-opera tearjerker, Moriarty and De Niro create a plausible bond, and the disease fades into the background as the Mammoths, and Pearson, go on a tear. By season's end, Pearson is too sick to accompany the team to the World Series; he dies that December. Wiggin is the only team member to attend the funeral. These are his last words, said in voiceover, as he strolls through the cemetery. They are also the last words in the novel, by Mark Harris, upon which the film is based.

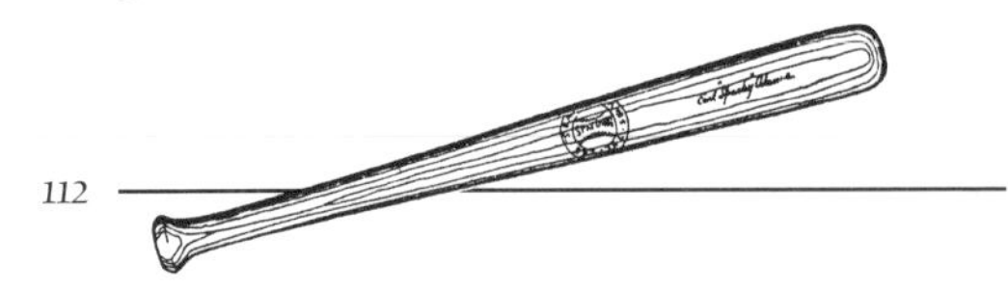

"Perhaps it's better if I live in your heart where the world can't see me. If I'm dead, there will be no stain on our love."

NAME: Marguerite Gautier
MOVIE: *Camille* (1936)
OCCUPATION: Courtesan

One of Hollywood's most potent early love films, *Camille* is based on Alexandre Dumas fils' 1848 novel, *La Dame aux Camelias.* The movie, directed by George Cukor, brings the doomed courtesan Marguerite Gautier (the beguiling Greta Garbo) and her hopelessly smitten client Armand Duval (Robert Taylor) together at film's end for a memorable death scene. Slowly dying of consumption while also having to accept the impossibility of a penniless prostitute's marriage to a moneyed young noble like Armand, Garbo portrays Marguerite in a fine performance enhanced by her husky voice, traces of a Scandinavian accent, and crisp, breathless enunciation of these famous last words. Just before these words are spoken, Armand bursts into the room, ready to toss away his social position in order to take her to the country and then to the altar. When she swoons in his arms, he calls for a doctor. She responds, "Doctor? If you can't make me live, how can he?" In the book, her famous last words are, "I can speak, but I am stifled when I speak; I am stifling. Air!"

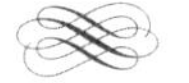

"I didn't believe hard enough. They won't let us be . . . "
"Then we'll get away."
"Yeah, we can, we will . . . "

NAMES: Tony and Maria
MOVIE: *West Side Story* (1961)
OCCUPATIONS: Gang member; girlfriend

In the frantic closing scenes of *West Side Story,* Tony (portrayed by Richard Beymer) is shot by rival gang members and dies in the arms of his girlfriend, Maria (Natalie Wood). As he dies, Maria begins singing the song "There's A Place for Us": "Hold my hand and we're halfway there / Hold my hand and I'll take you there / Somehow, someday . . . "—and then Tony is dead. The film (directed by Robert Wise and Jerome Robbins, who also did the choreography) won ten Academy Awards. The music was composed by Leonard Bernstein, with lyrics by Stephen Sondheim.

"Oh good . . . for a moment there I thought we were in trouble."

NAME: Butch Cassidy
MOVIE: *Butch Cassidy and the Sundance Kid* (1969)
OCCUPATION: Bank robber

Having worn out their welcome with the law back in the United States, Butch Cassidy (Paul Newman) and the Sundance Kid (Robert Redford) relocate to Bolivia. After a string of bank robberies there, they briefly try going straight. Then they learn that the tireless American lawman who had been tracking them back home has pursued them to South America. They have pulled one heist too many and are cornered in a flyblown Bolivian market town. Both seriously wounded and pinned down by gunfire, they reload their guns in anticipation of the next assault while hundreds of troops scramble into position outside. Although the situation is hopeless, they discuss their options. Butch suggests Australia. "It's a long way, though, isn't it?" asks the Kid. Butch snaps, "Ah, everything has got to be perfect with you." Suddenly he remembers the American lawman who has been tracking them and asks the Kid if he has seen him among the Bolivians outside. "No," the Kid says, to which Butch replies with these famous last words. He and the Sundance Kid leap out, their guns blazing, into a fatal hail of bullets.

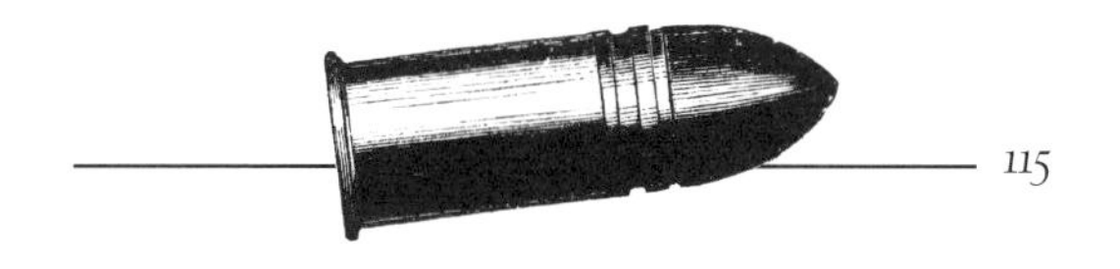

"Good morning, sir. This is my birthday. Give me the best in the house. . . . Thank you, sir."

NAME: J. B. Books
MOVIE: *The Shootist* (1976)
OCCUPATION: Gunslinger

These were the last words John Wayne said on screen, the last words in the last of his two hundred and fifty films. His character, J. B. Books, speaks them before being shot to death—by three men, including the bartender who served him his last drink—in a harrowing gunfight inside a Carson City saloon, circa 1901. The crusty Books is literally a dying breed, the last of the Old West's "shootists," whose credo is "I won't be wronged, I won't be insulted, I won't be laid a hand on." He has returned to Carson City, intending to spend his last days in peace, but the town has been "civilized" since his last visit, with horseless carriages, omnibuses, electric lights, telephones, and indoor plumbing. Books visits a doctor (played by equally creaky James Stewart) who has saved his life in the past; the doctor tells Books he has cancer (as Wayne had, in real life), gives him a supply of laudanum, and sends him to a comfortable boarding house run by Lauren Bacall. Rather than die in bed, Books faces death with dignity, so to speak, by defending himself against a gang of loathsome varmints in one final shootout.

"Tomorrow, I'll think of some way to get him back. After all, tomorrow is another day."

NAME: Scarlett O'Hara
MOVIE: *Gone with the Wind* (1939)
OCCUPATION: Southern belle

In adapting Margaret Mitchell's 1,037-page novel, published in 1936, to a screenplay, Sidney Howard focused on the steamy relationship between Scarlett O'Hara (Vivien Leigh) and Rhett Butler (Clark Gable). Even with such streamlining, the film—released in 1939—was the longest screen epic made in Hollywood to that date, at three hours, thirty-nine minutes in length. Scarlett O'Hara was given the honor of uttering the last words in the film, although most people remember more clearly Rhett Butler saying, just prior to her coda, "Frankly, my dear, I don't give a damn." Both Howard and Leigh won Academy Awards, and the film broke all previous box office records. A sobering note: while crossing an Atlanta street to see a movie at the same theater where *Gone with the Wind* had premiered ten years earlier, Margaret Mitchell (1900–1949) was hit and killed instantly by an off-duty cab driver. No last words were recorded.

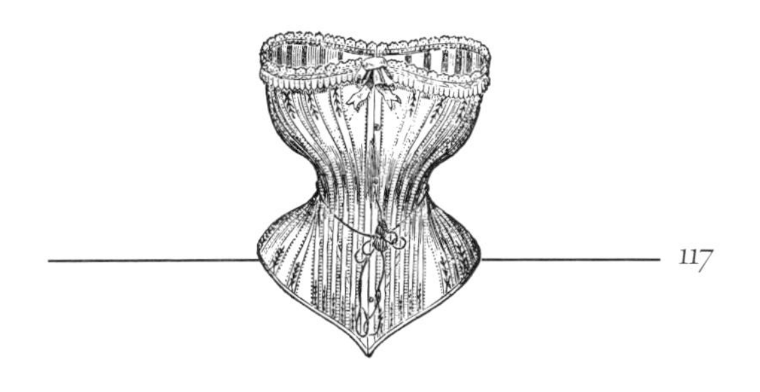

"*Mother of Mercy! Is this the end of Rico?*"

NAME: Rico (Cesare Enrico) Bandello
MOVIE: *Little Caesar* (1930)
OCCUPATION: Hoodlum

Sick of being a two-bit robber of gas stations, Rico Bandello (played by Edward G. Robinson) moves east and winnows his way into a mob faction run by Sam Vettori; he soon takes over Vettorri's Club Palermo gang. Howling "I want to be somebody," he then ruthlessly sets out to make that happen, rising to prominence via a massive ego, a need for the gratifications of expensive clothes and jewelry (but, oddly, no dames), an iron will, and an itchy trigger finger. The latter brings about his downfall: during a ballroom heist he kills the city's crime commissioner. The murder is eventually pinned on him. The gang is broken up, Vettori is hanged, and Rico ends up in a flophouse, drunk on his ass (it had been a point of honor that he never touched alcohol). After the stories circulate that he had turned "yellow" and couldn't "take it," Rico leads the cops into one last shootout. They machine-gun him as he takes cover behind a billboard. As he is dying, he says to Flaherty, his nemesis on the police force, "I told you no buzzard like you will ever put any cuffs on me." Then, he groans and offers these famous last words.

"It was fun."

NAME: James T. Kirk
TV SERIES: *Star Trek*
OCCUPATION: Captain of starship *Enterprise*

The last episode of the original *Star Trek* television series was filmed in January 1969 but not aired on NBC until June 3 of that year. The hour-long drama, called "Turnabout Intruder," required Kirk (played by William Shatner) to act out the parts of both a male and female personality, the latter having been transferred to his body telepathically by a paranoiac scientist, Dr. Janice Lester, who Captain Kirk had rejected years earlier. The ratings for the episode, up against CBS's *Lancer* and ABC's *Mod Squad*—each of which nearly doubled its viewership—were half of what *Star Trek* attracted during its heyday. Thought dead at the time, the show gained a new life in syndicated reruns, and eventually three entirely new *Star Trek* television series were created, as well as several feature-length films starring members of the original cast.

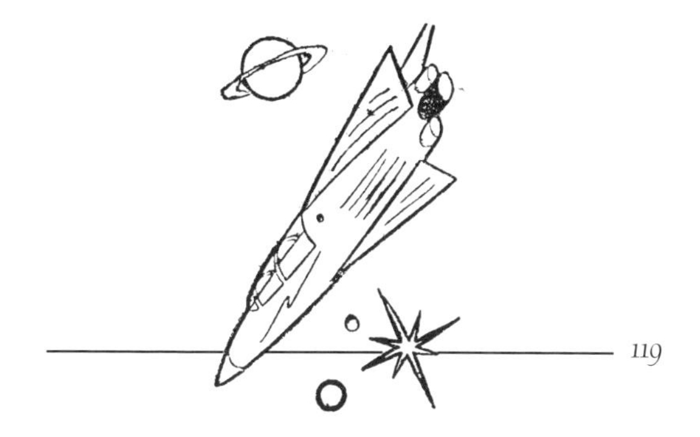

"I can only tell you it has been an honor and a privilege to come into your homes. I hope when I find something I want to do and I think you will like and come back, you'll be as gracious in inviting me into your homes as you have been. I bid you a very heartfelt goodnight."

NAME: Johnny Carson
TV SERIES: *The Tonight Show*
OCCUPATION: Talk show host

Rather than having a star-studded, guest-filled final show, Carson just reminisced about "favorite moments" with sidekicks Ed McMahon and Doc Severinson. Carson estimated that since his debut on October 1, 1962 (with Groucho Marx as guest), he had walked through the curtain over five thousand times and hosted twenty-four thousand guests. He joked about "taking the APPLAUSE sign home and putting it in my bedroom." Just before imparting these final words on May 22, 1992, he said, "I'm one of the lucky people in the world. I've found something I always wanted to do and I've enjoyed every single minute of it." Carson's farewell signaled an end to a kind of broadcasting that cut across age, race, gender, and class to create a sense of national community.

Chapter Seven

On the Page

"It's a wonder I haven't abandoned all my ideals, they seem so absurd and impractical. Yet I cling to them because I still believe, in spite of everything, that people are truly good at heart."

NAME: Anne Frank
YEARS OF LIFE: 1929–1945
OCCUPATION: Diarist

This is among the last entries from the diary of Anne Frank: her family's hiding place in occupied Amsterdam was discovered by Nazis on August 1, 1944. She began her chronicle on June 12, 1942, a thirteen-year-old girl excited by a birthday gift, her diary—"You were the first thing I saw, maybe one of my nicest presents." Over the next two years, she described her Jewish family's life in Het Achterhuis (the House Behind), her emotional hopes and fears, spiritual and physical longings, passions, and humor. What would probably have been a glowing career as a writer was cut short at the death camp at Bergen-Belsen, where she and her sister died of typhus. Anne Frank had intimations of her own mortality. Three sentences after this hopeful, often-quoted excerpt, she wrote, "I hear the approaching thunder that, one day, will destroy us too." Her manuscript was published as *Diary of a Young Girl* in 1947.

"Shakespeare, here I come!"

NAME: Theodore Dreiser
YEARS OF LIFE: 1871–1945
OCCUPATION: Writer

Controversial, combative, and proud, Theodore Dreiser (whose works include *Sister Carrie* and *An American Tragedy*) chose this self-mocking, self-aggrandizing exclamation to be his last words, years before he died. While such gestures were an outgrowth of a volcanic ego, Dreiser had valid reasons for being belligerent. One of thirteen children, he grew up in abject poverty, and trouble pursued him (when he wasn't pursuing it) throughout his life. Although critically praised, his novels did not sell especially well, and several were suppressed for their bleakly naturalistic, "adult" themes. It figures that Dreiser would console himself, even if in jest, with the idea that his writing would long outlive his angry, unhappy life. He could have easily died much sooner. In 1912, he had booked passage on the *Titanic,* but at the last minute he switched to the *Kroonland* because the fare was considerably cheaper.

"My children, I do not see very clearly now, I had some things more to say, but it makes no difference. Think of me a little. You are blessed creatures. I do not know what is the matter with me, I see a light. Come nearer. I die happy. Let me put my hands upon your dear beloved heads."

NAME: Jean Valjean
NOVEL: *Les Misérables* (1862)
OCCUPATION: Convict; advocate for the poor
AUTHOR: Victor Hugo (1802–1885)

At his death as a feeble old man, Jean Valjean, the former convict turned "foster-father of the poor," is reunited with Cosette, the daughter of Fantine, a woman he had helped years earlier. Marius, Cosette's husband, is also there. Valjean feels that if he is to die happy, he must first secure their forgiveness for a crime that he committed to feed his sister's starving children. He also assures Cosette of her inherited fortune from the glasswork technique that he has invented, and observes, "It is nothing to die; it is frightful not to live." After motioning for them to bend closer to the bed, Valjean's last words take up two pages, a loving, rambling reminiscence and, finally, a gentle farewell.

"It is a far, far better thing that I do, than I have ever done: it is a far, far better rest that I go to, than I have ever known."

NAME: Sidney Carton
NOVEL: *A Tale of Two Cities* (1859)
OCCUPATION: Barrister
AUTHOR: Charles Dickens (1812–1870)

While Charles Dickens wrote the installments for *A Tale of Two Cities,* serialized in *All the Year Round,* events in his own life mirrored those he put on paper. "What is done and suffered in these pages," he wrote, "I have certainly done and suffered . . . myself." He admitted to a friend, in fact, that he longed to play the part of Sidney Carton on stage. Carton, who utters this famous closing line in the novel, is the hero who willingly dies on the guillotine to save the life of a rival for the love of Lucie Manette. At the time, Dickens was estranged from his wife, Catherine, and involved with protracted legal proceedings regarding their children. This undoubtedly colored the writing of his tale of revolution, turning it into a meditation on redemption through selfless death.

"But watch out for that ambulance. We don't want to begin our pilgrimage with an accident."

NAME: Ignatius J. Reilly
NOVEL: *A Confederacy of Dunces* (1980)
OCCUPATION: File clerk; hotdog-pushcart man
AUTHOR: John Kennedy Toole (1937–1969)

The manuscript of *A Confederacy of Dunces* was found among writer and teacher John Kennedy Toole's papers by his mother after her son committed suicide. She brought the manscript to novelist Walker Percy, who realized it was "a fantastic novel, a major achievement, a huge comic-satiric-tragic one-of-a-kind rendering . . . a great rumbling farce of Falstaffian dimensions." Indeed, the book, not published until 1980, won the Pulitzer Prize and established itself as a masterwork of comedy. Percy described Toole's protagonist, Ignatius J. Reilly, as "a slob extraordinary, a mad Oliver Hardy, a fat Don Quixote, a perverse Thomas Aquinas rolled into one—who is in violent revolt against the entire modern age." As he makes his final escape from that world, with the aid of love interest Myrna Minkoff ("the musky minx"), Ignatius offers these words of advice about her driving.

"Well, Nelson, all I can tell you is, it isn't so bad."

NAME: Harry (Rabbit) Angstrom
NOVEL: *Rabbit at Rest* (1990)
OCCUPATION: Car salesman; basketball star
AUTHOR: John Updike (b. 1932)

Although John Updike is one of America's most prolific literary figures, his creation of the Harry "Rabbit" Angstrom books—a tetralogy that spans four decades—may be his greatest accomplishment. Regardless of one's feelings about him, Rabbit is undeniably one of the most fully realized characters in American literature. A former high school basketball star, Rabbit is part rogue, part romantic: hapless and hopeless and occasionally happy. By the time his heart gives out at the end of *Rabbit at Rest,* he is prepared to tell his son Nelson that he has a sister, born illegitimately to another woman. However, hearing his son cry, "Don't die, Dad, don't!", Rabbit finds that he can only console him with these, the last words in Updike's classic creation.

"So we beat on, boats against the current, borne back ceaselessly into the past."

NAME: Nick Carraway
NOVEL: *The Great Gatsby* (1925)
OCCUPATION: Bonds dealer
AUTHOR: F. Scott Fitzgerald (1896–1949)

The last words in Fitzgerald's *The Great Gatsby* are spoken by the book's narrator. They are also chiseled into the headstone of Fitzgerald's grave in Rockville, Maryland, where he lies buried beside his wife, Zelda Sayre Fitzgerald. Jay Gatsby was a bootlegger who dreamed of being one of the beautiful people, like Daisy Buchanan, with whom he was obsessed. Before Daisy married Tom Buchanan, she had been briefly involved with Gatsby. He fails to win Daisy in the end, which makes his death at the hands of another wounded man, gas station attendant George B. Wilson, seem inevitable. As Nick put it, "Tom and Daisy—they smashed up things and creatures and then retreated back into their money or their vast carelessness, or whatever it was that kept them together, and let other people clean up the mess they had made. . . ."

"That's well said, but we must cultivate our garden."

NAME: Candide
NOVEL: *Candide, or Optimism* (1759)
OCCUPATION: Naïve philosopher
AUTHOR: Voltaire (François Marie Arouet de; 1694–1778)

Candide, a simpleminded but honest and gentle boy, was brought up in the castle of Baron Thunder-ten-tronckh in Westphalia. His rosy view of the world was shaped by the court philosopher, Doctor Pangloss. A typical Panglossian observation: "'Tis demonstrated that things cannot be otherwise; for, since everything is made for an end, everything is necessarily for the best end. Observe that noses were made to wear spectacles; and so we have spectacles." After Candide is expelled from the "noble castle," he is put through a series of arduous, preposterous struggles—from unrequited love to the brutalities of the Inquisition—which sorely test his view that this is "the best of all possible worlds." At the end, reduced to eking out an existence as a farmer, Candide seems to have developed a more pragmatic worldview. After Pangloss, with whom he has been reunited, assures him that "all events are linked up in this best of all possible worlds," Candide offers these parting words.

"Like a dog!"

NAME: Joseph K.
NOVEL: *The Trial* (1925, tr. 1937)
OCCUPATION: Bank bureaucrat
AUTHOR: Franz Kafka (1883–1924)

Joseph K., a quiet and respectable functionary at a bank, is arrested one morning. The Inspector and entourage who come to the boardinghouse where he lives will not state the reason for his arrest, nor will they tell him under whose authority the arrest is being made. Joseph K.'s orderly life is thrown into chaos by this event, although he consoles himself with thoughts like "Who could these men be? What were they talking about? What authority could they represent?" K. lives in a country with a legal constitution, there is universal peace, all the laws are in force—"Who dares seize him in his dwelling?" What ensues is a nightmarish plunge into an increasingly baffling bureaucracy. Eventually K. is sentenced to die. He allows the two strangers to hold him down, plunge the knife into his heart, and turn it twice. He hurls the words "Like a dog!" into their faces, "as if he meant the shame of it to outlive him."

"Pardon me 'Krazy'. Pardon me. I'll save you. Here I come."

NAME: Offisa Pupp
COMIC STRIP: *Krazy Kat* (1913–1944)
CREATOR: George Herriman (1880–1944)

These were the last words in the last printed episode of the great comic strip *Krazy Kat*. Herriman's inventive language, bizarre characters (with even more bizarre character flaws), and surrealistic settings set new standards for comic strip art. In fact, few have ever approached Herriman for consistency of invention. His main characters were Krazy Kat, who was in love with Ignatz Mouse, who heaves bricks at him (or her) with remarkable and painful accuracy (serving only to make the Kat's obsessive love stronger). Offisa Pupp, oblivious to the Kat's infatuation with the Mouse and to the Mouse's "artistry with the bricks," is entrusted with maintaining order in Herriman's strip. In the final panel, published two months after Herriman's death, Pupp pulls Kat from a pool and cradles him to his chest while Mouse looks on—perplexed, sad, angry, maybe even jealous.

"Dear Friends, I have been fortunate to draw Charlie Brown and his friends for almost fifty years. It has been the fulfillment of my childhood ambition. Unfortunately, I am no longer able to maintain the schedule demanded by a daily comic strip. My family does not wish Peanuts to be continued by anyone else, therefore I am announcing my retirement. I have been grateful over the years for the loyalty of our editors and the wonderful support and love expressed to me by fans of the comic strip. Charlie Brown, Snoopy, Linus, Lucy . . . how can I ever forget them."

NAME: Charles M. Schulz
CARTOON STRIP: *Peanuts* (1950–2000)
CREATOR: Charles M. Schulz (1922–2000)

By the time the last daily installment of *Peanuts* appeared on January 3, 2000, Charles Schulz's beloved strip was syndicated in 2,400 newspapers in sixty-eight countries. Suffering from colon cancer and recovering from surgery in November 1999, Schulz announced that he would retire to spend time with his family. Unexpected was the abruptness of the gentle cartoonist's death, on February 12, 2000. The final *Peanuts* strip opens with Charlie Brown saying into a telephone, "No, I think he's writing." Snoopy is then seen atop his doghouse, pecking out a letter that serves as the strip's, and Schulz's, famous last words. The letter is quoted here in full.

“mayonnaise”

NAME: Richard Brautigan
NOVEL: *Trout Fishing in America* (1967)
YEARS OF LIFE: 1935–1984
OCCUPATION: Writer

Richard Brautigan was an American original whose prose and poetry were cut from the same offbeat, unpredictable cloth: bowling trophies and mine disasters, Kool-Aid winos and Confederate generals. As a San Franciscan during a time of great countercultural activity in that city, Brautigan became associated with the flower children, and his gentle dispatches—like R. Crumb's cartoons—were passed from hand to hand. His best-known book was a “novel” called *Trout Fishing in America,* which was not necessarily about trout fishing. In the second to last chapter, he writes, “Expressing a human need, I always wanted to write a book that ended with the word Mayonnaise.” So, he ends the final chapter (called “The Mayonnaise Chapter”) in this manner: “P. S. Sorry I forgot to give you the mayonnaise.”

"The horror! The horror!"

NAME: Mr. Kurtz
NOVEL: *Heart of Darkness* (1902)
OCCUPATION: Businessman
AUTHOR: Joseph Conrad (born Józef Teodor Konrad Korzeniowski; 1857–1924)

Joseph Conrad based the events in his short novel *Heart of Darkness* on an 1890 trip he made as a British seaman into the interior of the Congo. Marlowe, the novel's narrator, is hired by an ivory-trading firm to take a boat into the jungle to check on Mr. Kurtz, the firm's top agent. It is rumored that Kurtz has gone mad or turned into a savage, or both. When Marlowe finds him, Kurtz is, indeed, diseased in mind, body, and spirit. His "fiefdom" is littered with dead and mutilated bodies; his victims' heads adorn the fenceposts around his house. Marlowe manages to get Kurtz on the boat and begins the voyage out of the darkness and back to "civilization." Kurtz dies on the journey, not before screaming, "The horror! The horror!" Among Kurtz's effects Marlowe has found a report that the agent had written, "to be presented to the International Society for the Suppression of Savage Customs." At the end of the report Kurtz had scrawled, "Exterminate all the brutes!"

"But soon, I shall die, and what I now feel be no longer felt. Soon these burning miseries will be extinct. I shall ascend my funeral pile triumphantly and exult in the agony of the torturing flames. The light of that conflagration will fade away; my ashes will be swept into the sea by the winds. My spirit will sleep in peace, or if it thinks, it will not surely think thus. Farewell."

NAME: Unnamed "daemon"
NOVEL: *Frankenstein, or The Modern Prometheus* (1818)
AUTHOR: Mary Shelley
YEARS OF LIFE: 1797–1851

A philosophy student, Frankenstein discovers the secret of bestowing life on inanimate matter. He forms a human from bones and flesh gathered from charnel houses and brings it to life, but the hideous-looking gentle giant terrifies all who see him. Unable to find "love and fellowship," the monster seeks revenge against Frankenstein by murdering his brother. When the monster learns that despite this tragedy, Frankenstein still plans to wed, he murders the intended bride. Frankenstein goes after the monster, intending to destroy him; he finds him in the Arctic. The monster murders his creator, and then proclaims these last words to Frankenstein's companion.

"They are loaded. The clock strikes twelve! So be it, then! Lotte! Lotte! Farewell! Farewell!"

NAME: Werther
NOVEL: *The Sorrows of Young Werther* (1774)
OCCUPATION: Student
AUTHOR: Johann Wolfgang von Goethe (1749–1832)

Goethe's depiction of his tragic hero was based on the suicide of Karl Wilhelm Jerusalem, a close friend from his student days. Like Jerusalem, Werther feels snubbed by aristocrats, alienated from conventional society, and in despair over an unhappy (and unrequited) love for a married woman. Like Goethe, Werther was born August 28, has a pantheistic love of nature, admires Homer, and is passionately attached to an unavailable woman. In Goethe's story of Werther's final days—as told in a series of letters from the sorrowful young man—the woman is Lotte, who is engaged to Albert, a man groomed for success. Werther's delusional hope that the marriage will not happen is soon dashed when the two are betrothed, and his despair becomes unbearable. His final letter to Lotte goes on for pages, but these are its last words. Goethe's novel created an instant sensation in Europe. The "Werther costume" (blue-tailed coat, yellow waistcoat, high boots) became a fashion statement, and a rash of copycat suicides among other sensitive young men were reported.

"Hush, Mas'r George!—it worries me! Don't feel so! He an't done me no real harm,—only opened the gate of the kingdom for me; that's all! Who,—who,—who shall separate us from the love of Christ?"

NAME: Uncle Tom
NOVEL: *Uncle Tom's Cabin* (1852)
OCCUPATION: Slave
AUTHOR: Harriet Beecher Stowe (1811–1896)

Master George has shown up at Tom's bedside to purchase him from Simon Legree and take him back to Kentucky. But, as Tom tells "Mas'r George," "Ye're too late. The Lord's bought me, and is going to take me home, —and I long to go. Heaven is better than Kintuck." Even as George curses Legree as "the old satan," Tom makes it clear he forgives the "poor mis'able critter" who has made his own existence a living hell. His last words are, in fact, almost a prayer of thanks for the suffering that Legree has inflicted on him, since it has made him spiritually strong and ready for death.

"Thou art the last of our race, the Waegmundings. Fate has swept off all my kinsfolk, undaunted nobles, to their doom, I must go after them."

NAME: Beowulf
POEM: "Beowulf" (c. sixth century)
OCCUPATION: King of the Geats

"Beowulf" is the earliest epic poem in any "modern" language, dating to the tenth century in written form and perhaps to as early as the sixth century in oral form. It recounts the heroic deeds of Beowulf, the nephew of Higelac, king of the Geats (a tribe of southern Sweden). Hearing about the troubles visited on the Danes by the monster Grendel, Beowulf sails with fourteen companions to offer help. He fights and mortally wounds Grendel, tearing off the monster's arm. Grendel's mother seeks revenge; Beowulf beheads her (and beheads Grendel's corpse for good measure), wins riches, and rules the Geats for the next fifty years. A dragon begins to lay waste to Beowulf's kingdom, so the hero goes out to do battle with the fire-breathing beast, which is guarding a huge treasure. Beowulf kills the dragon, with Wiglaf's help, but he himself receives a fatal wound. Before Beowulf speaks these words to Wiglaf, he gives the "thane, the young spear-warrior" his golden collar, his "gold-mounted" helmet, ring, and corslet, "and bade him use them well."

"Mostly, I'd just like to look over the country around the gorge again, just to bring some of it clear in my mind again. I been away a long time."

NAME: Broom Bromden
NOVEL: *One Flew over the Cuckoo's Nest* (1962)
OCCUPATION: Native American patient in a state mental hospital
AUTHOR: Ken Kesey (b. 1935)

Broom Bromden, a very tall Native American presumed to be a deaf mute, for years has been pushing a broom around the ward. His placid world is disturbed by the arrival of Randall McMurphy, who has avoided prison by faking insanity. Until his arrival, no one dared upset the ward's balance of power: Nurse Ratched (aka Big Nurse) rules with totalitarian efficiency. The novel, whose authenticity derives from Kesey's experience as a mental hospital orderly, details the test of wills between Big Nurse and McMurphy, who is a catalyst through whom Broom connects again to his legacy and memories of his father, once a chief. McMurphy gets the ultimate punishment: a lobotomy. Unable to bear seeing his liberator reduced to helplessness, Broom suffocates McMurphy with a pillow. Suddenly restored to full strength, Broom smashes a barred security window and escapes, heading back to his tribal homeland, saying these last words.

"The blind man!"

NAME: Emma Bovary
NOVEL: *Madame Bovary* (1857)
OCCUPATION: Romantic; adulteress; debtor
AUTHOR: Gustave Flaubert (1821–1880)

Outside the window of the room where Emma waits to die from self-poisoning, the sound of "heavy wooden shoes and the scraping of a stick" can be heard, followed by a raucous voice singing a naughty song that ends with "The wind blew very hard that day / And snatched her petticoat away!" Emma's revery of eternal bliss—she has just taken communion—is interrupted by this visitation from her past. She "began to laugh—a horrible, frantic, desperate laugh—fancying that she saw the beggar's hideous face, a figure of terror looming up in the darkness of eternity." When her sudden pang of recognition and her desperate laugh are over, she has "ceased to exist."

CHAPTER EIGHT

By One's Own Hand

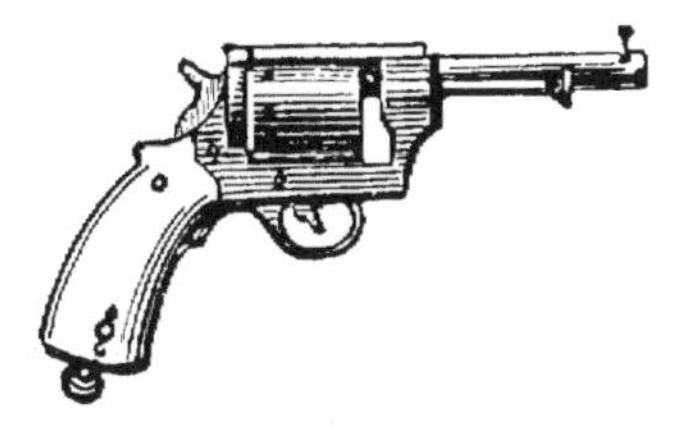

"I wish my friends to know that I am leaving their company in a peaceful frame of mind, with some timid hopes for a depersonalised afterlife beyond due confines of space, time, and matter and beyond the limits of our comprehension. This 'oceanic feeling' has often sustained me at difficult moments, and does so now, while I am writing this."

NAME: Arthur Koestler
YEARS OF LIFE: 1905–1983
OCCUPATON: Writer

Arthur Koestler, author of a classic novel of totalitarianism, *Darkness at Noon,* and an assortment of nonfiction works, began a steady physical decline in his later years. When it reached what he called an "acute state," he wrote a farewell message explaining why he found it "advisable to seek self-deliverance now." This lengthy suicide note, the last part of which is contained here, was completed in June 1982. Koestler and his wife, Cynthia, ingested lethal amounts of barbiturates and died on March 1, 1983. Cynthia Koestler was only fifty-seven years old and in good health. She appended this odd note at the end of the farewell message: "I should have liked to finish my account of working for Arthur . . . However, I cannot live without Arthur, despite certain inner resources."

"If I had one single point of character or goodness I would stand on that and grow back to life."

NAME: Marian (Clover) Hooper Adams
YEARS OF LIFE: 1843–1885
OCCUPATION: Amateur photographer; hostess

During her thirteen years of idyllic marriage to the renowned historian Henry Adams, Clover Adams—the product of two of Boston's most esteemed families (Hooper and Sturgis)—was much admired as a lively and intelligent woman. The Adamses were in demand at all the society and literary events, and their house was the center of Washington, D.C., high society. When her beloved father, Robert Hooper, died in early 1885, Clover fell into an intractable depression. Among her few confidantes was her sister, Ellen, to whom she wrote her last letter—cited here—explaining why she was committing suicide. After her death, Henry Adams, who lived until 1918, could not bear to mention her name and did not even mention her in his autobiography, *The Education of Henry Adams.* He was buried alongside Clover in Rock Creek Cemetery, beneath the famous scupture he had commissioned for her by Auguste Sainte-Gaudens.

"I have just had to tell your mother that I shall be dead in a quarter of an hour. Hitler is charging me with high treason. In view of my services in Africa I am to have the chance of dying by poison. The two generals have brought it with them. It is fatal in three seconds. If I accept, none of the usual steps will be taken against my family. I'm to be given a state funeral. It's all been prepared to the last detail. In a quarter of an hour you will receive a call from the hospital in Ulm to say that I've had a brain seizure on the way to a conference."

NAME: Erwin Rommel
YEARS OF LIFE: 1891–1944
OCCUPATION: Field marshal

On July 20, 1944, Colonel Count von Stauffenberg planted a time bomb beneath the conference table at Wolf's Lair, Adolf Hitler's headquarters. The colonel was one of a large group of high-level German military officers who were desperate to end the war and Hitler's insane rule. They had even formed an anti-Nazi government to rule after Hitler's death, hoping to negotiate peace with the Allies. The highest-ranking officer involved was Field Marshal Rommel, Hitler's favorite general and Germany's most popular military leader, affectionately known as the Desert Rat. When the bomb failed to kill Hitler, the Gestapo extracted vicious retribution: 4,980 of the 7,000 people arrested were executed. Due to his status, Rommel was given the option of taking poison; the note excerpted above explained the situation to his son Manfred. Hitler kept his promise, even wiring Frau Rommel: "Accept my sincerest sympathy for the heavy loss you have suffered with the death of your husband." At Rommel's funeral, the oration concluded, "His heart belonged to the Fuehrer."

"Dearest, I want to tell you that you have given me complete happiness. No one could have done more than you have done. Please believe that. But I know that I shall never get over this: & I am wasting your life. It is this madness. Nothing anyone says can persuade me. You can work, & you will be much better without me. You see I can't write this even, which shows I am right. All I want to say is that until this disease came on we were perfectly happy. It was all due to you. No one could have been so good as you have been. From the very first day till now. Everyone knows that . . . You will find Roger's letters to the Maurons in the writing table drawer in the Lodge. Will you destroy all my papers."

Name: Virginia Woolf
Years of Life: 1882–1941
Occupation: Writer

In the spring of 1941, having finished a draft of the novel *Between the Acts,* Virginia Woolf began to exhibit signs of mental fatigue. Her husband, Leonard, confessed, in a letter to her editor John Lehmann, "she is on the verge of a complete nervous break down and is seriously ill." Leonard made arrangements for her to see a doctor and was in the process of arranging a "rest cure" for her. But before he could do so, she arranged a rest of a different kind. On March 28, 1941, Woolf wrote a final letter to her husband, left it in a blue envelope, and walked out to the River Ouse. She put a large stone in her pocket, dropped her walking stick, and walked into the fast-moving water. She could not swim.

❦

"I have it good, and I'm grateful, but since the age of seven, I've become hateful towards all humans in general. Only because it seems so easy for people to get along that have empathy. Only because I love and feel sorry for people too much, I guess. Thank you all from the pit of my burning, nauseous stomach for your letters and concern during the past years. I'm too much of an erratic, moody baby! I don't have the passion anymore, and so remember, it's better to burn out than to fade away. Peace, love, empathy, Kurt Cobain. Frances and Courtney, I'll be at your altar. Please keep going Courtney, for Frances. For her life, which will be so much happier without me. I love you, I love you."

NAME: Kurt Donald Cobain
YEARS OF LIFE: 1967–1994
OCCUPATION: Musician

Kurt Cobain fronted the three-piece rock band Nirvana, the most successful of the many excellent bands that came out of Seattle's "grunge" scene. Nirvana's music, written and sung by Cobain, won a loyal following among tens of thousands of disaffected fans. Cobain came from a broken home and was brutalized by adults as a child. Whatever else may have contributed to his suicide—including a tempestuous marriage to Courtney Love; abuse of heroin and other chemicals—it seems that the success of his band and his own sudden wealth filled him with shame and remorse. He was found dead on April 8, 1994, of a self-inflicted gunshot wound, along with his long suicide note (of which these are just the last few lines), in a room of his large but nearly empty Seattle "mansion."

"Human life is limited; but I would like to live forever."

NAME: Yukio Mishima (born Hiraoka Kimitake)
YEARS OF LIFE: 1925–1970
OCCUPATION: Writer

Mishima was born in Tokyo into a samurai family and adhered all his life to the rigid principles embodied by that tradition. He engaged in rigorous physical fitness regimens, practiced the ancient arts of karate and swordsmanship, and warned against the softening of Japanese culture in the face of postwar materialism. The leading cultural figure in postwar Japan, Mishima was a prolific writer of novels, stories, essays, and plays, as well as taking starring roles on stage and screen. As Japan drifted further from the principles that he espoused, he grew increasingly despondent and disgusted. He attempted to overthrow the civil government, taking over a military headquarters in Tokyo and exhorting the armed forces to seize the country. When this failed, Mishima committed the ritual disembowelment called *seppuku* with a samurai sword. One of his closest friends was entrusted with the task of beheading him (also part of the ritual samurai suicide). He spoke the words above just before the blade came down.

"When I am dead, and over me bright April
Shakes out her rain drenched hair,
Tho you should lean above me broken hearted,
I shall not care.
For I shall have peace.
As leafy trees are peaceful
When rain bends down the bough.
And I shall be more silent and cold hearted
Than you are now."

NAME: Sara Teasdale
YEARS OF LIFE: 1884–1933
OCCUPATION: Poet

Sara Teasdale made her name as a poet in connection with a literary circle in Chicago that included Vachel Lindsay, with whom she carried on a long courtship. After breaking off her engagement with Lindsay, she married a St. Louis businessman in 1914; the marriage was unhappy, and she divorced him in Reno in 1929. Lindsay's 1931 suicide affected her deeply; for the last two years of her life Teasdale was increasingly despondent. She became involved with a younger man whose disinterest precipitated her final crisis. Before taking an overdose of sleeping pills and drowning in her bathtub, Teasdale wrote this angry, sorrowful poem as her suicide note, presumably intended for the man she felt had rejected her.

Bibliography

Bulfinch, Thomas. *Myths of Greece and Rome.* New York: Viking Penguin, 1979.

Durant, Will. *The Story of Civilization.* Volumes I–VI. New York: Simon and Schuster, 1954–1957.

Durant, Will and Ariel Durant. *The Story of Civilization.* Volumes VII–XI. New York: Simon and Schuster, 1961–1975.

Evans, Harold. *The American Century.* New York: Alfred A. Knopf, 1998.

Foner, Eric and John A. Garraty, eds. *The Reader's Companion to American History.* Boston: Houghton Mifflin, 1991.

Grene, David and Richard Lattimore, eds. *The Complete Greek Tragedies,* vols. I–IV. Chicago: The University of Chicago Press, 1959.

Harvey, Sir Paul. *The Oxford Companion to English Literature.* New York: Oxford University Press, 1945

Hochschild, Adam. *King Leopold's Ghost.* Boston: Houghton Mifflin, 1998.

Katz, Ephraim. *The Film Encyclopedia.* New York: Harper Perennial, 1994.

Kunitz, Stanley J. and Howard Haycraft, eds. *Twentieth Century Authors: A Biographical Dictionary of Modern Literature.* New York: H. W. Wilson Co., 1942.

Ruffin, C. Bernard. *Last Words: A Dictionary of Deathbed Quotations.* Jefferson, NC: McFarland & Co., 1995

Name Index